KEEP OUT!
BRITAIN'S FORBIDDEN PLACES

Edward Couzens-Lake

AMBERLEY

First published 2020

Amberley Publishing
The Hill, Stroud
Gloucestershire, GL5 4EP

www.amberleybooks.com

British Library Cataloguing in Publication Data.
A catalogue record for this book is available from the British Library.

ISBN 978 1 4456 7424 7 (print)
ISBN 978 1 4456 7425 4 (ebook)

Typeset in 10pt on 13pt Sabon.
Typesetting by SJmagic DESIGN SERVICES, India.
Printed in the UK.

Contents

Introduction

The US Government have got it all wrong with Area 51.

How easy would it be to keep Dreamland out of the public eye and, in doing so, remove any and all of the countless conspiracy theories that surround it, if they'd just littered the perimeter with a few rusting parts from a John Deere tractor, a few discarded tins of Budweiser and a closed down petrol station (sorry, gas station) complete with a screen door that is forever rattling back on its hinges in the unforgiving desert breeze?

No signs, no barbed wire, no patrolling guards or mysterious black helicopters forever prowling its perimeter. They needn't have bothered with any of that. If only they'd thought about it and dumped some twenty-first century detritus about the place. Had they done, no-one would have been the slightest bit interested in an otherwise obscure tract of Nevada desert and they could all have got on with their experiments with time travel and reverse engineering alien spacecraft without being bothered by anyone.

But no. They had to make it look like someplace where strange things happen, and on a regular basis. This meant that, as inevitably as night follows day, everyone immediately wanted to know just what the hell is going on up there? Because the more that someone – anyone – tries to cover something up, the more we want – we demand – to know everything there is to know about it, despite the fact that there are people out there who are absolutely determined that we don't.

It's that same compelling quirk of human nature that demands that, upon seeing a sign that says, 'Wet Paint', you just have to dab a finger or two on it to see if the sign is factually correct. And I bet I'm not the only one who has reached out and touched an otherwise innocuous looking fence just because it happens to have a notice on it that proclaims, 'Danger, This Fence Is Electrified'.

Our natural instinct, if we are told not to do something, is to get out there and do it anyway. It's programmed into us as children and, for many, it simply refuses to go away.

Hence the twin fascination with the secret, the forbidden, the unknown and the exclusive. The more secret something is made, the more forbidden any access or information regarding to it becomes, the more unknown and mysterious it is … the more we want to know. While if something is simply regarded as 'exclusive', which translates, more often than not, into a polite way of saying that whatever it is, the likes of you and I can never go there, well that just rankles and makes me want to go there anyway. Even if I don't like fishing.

I've selected forty different places in Great Britain that, one way or the other, manage to fit into one of those categories.

Such is the parlous state of the world that we live in today that many of them are related to the defence of the realm and, with that in mind, are probably places that we would never want to explore anyway. Yet, for all that, the fascination remains.

Others are rather more exclusive in that the reason most of us will never get past the front door is simply because of who we are, or, rather, who we aren't. While others are just a bit quirky in nature. And we all love a bit of quirkiness here.

Whatever it is, it won't stop us looking in from the outside, which is exactly what we are going to do in these pages. So, come and join me, let's touch all of that wet paint!

Foreword

As someone with a rigorous scientific training and heightened sense of curiosity, I've often had a yearning to walk free and unchallenged around some of the country's secret establishments, to get first-hand insight of what's going on behind their walls. Of course, most of us will never be able to enter such locations, unless it's your place of work and you have achieved sufficient security clearance. Otherwise, attempted access is likely to lead to severe and damaging personal repercussions.

The fact that I can't enter the corridors, offices and laboratories of these places doesn't exactly keep me awake at night, but now and again it is a source of some irritation that my professional career went in a direction which didn't bring the necessary privilege to allow for such a private tour.

Thankfully, my friend and author Edward Couzens-Lake shares my fascination and curiosity in this regard. Consequently, I was delighted when I discovered his intention to investigate further and publish his findings and chuffed to be asked to write this foreword. He's hand-picked forty such forbidden/restricted locations from across the land, describing what their primary function is and why we're not allowed to access the juicy details of what lurks behind the solid, forbidding facades and, in many cases, barbed wire, warning signs and security guards.

Alas, there is a variety of reasons why ordinary members of the general public such as you and I are not welcome to poke our inquisitive noses around certain buildings and establishments in England. Whether they are highly secretive in nature (e.g. government research facilities), restricted or secured private areas (away from prying eyes) of otherwise publicly accessible buildings, or those open only to fortunate folk with sufficient funds and influence far beyond yours or mine (e.g. private, fee-paying membership-only clubs or organisations), by nature such a lack of general access just makes us 'outsiders' even more determined to find out what we're missing out on.

Most commonly, the reason for an entrance rebuff is official secrecy i.e. the protection of sensitive data as determined by law – a frustrating barrier I know, but invariably a sensible precaution against the viewing and deliberate or unwitting dissemination of highly sensitive information to others with less innocent intentions than perhaps ourselves. Places where such high-level rules apply include government defence/weapon research facilities, for example the Atomic Weapons Establishment (AWE), Aldermaston or the Porton Down science park in Salisbury. Other types of highly secretive areas include military bases, weapon storage sites and nuclear bunkers, intelligence/security services (GCHQ, Cheltenham) as well as bioscience research facilities, such as Huntingdon Life Sciences in Cambridgeshire; the site of controversial research which has attracted public interest and condemnation in recent years. These and other examples are to be found in the twenty-five subjects of this work.

Not all of England's forbidden places/areas fall into this secrecy category, however. Other less sensitive information-based reasons are in play for denial of access.

For example, the author also discusses some of the most exclusive private membership clubs e.g. the All England Lawn Tennis and Croquet Club in Wimbledon, where primarily birth, social and financial factors tend to allow access to areas other than those available to the general public at only certain times of the year. Other highlighted examples falling in this 'privileged' category are the very exclusive Queenswood Golf Club in Surrey, where membership will set you back a small fortune, and White's Gentleman's Club in central London, where all sorts of privileged indulgences and practices no doubt occur beyond the gaze and knowledge of us mere mortals.

Now, let the author offer you a sneaky peek into this intriguing, yet infuriatingly veiled world of secrecy and privilege.

Dr Russell Saunders (PhD)

1. Aldermaston, Berkshire

Atomic Weapons Research Establishment

Ever heard of the Ministry of Supply (MoS)?

The MoS was formed in 1939 in order to coordinate the supply of equipment to each of the British Armed Forces, a decision that was, of course, taken with the prospect of war on a near global basis fast approaching as the year progressed.

It's said that nothing aids the advance of technology quite like a war, the advent of which has a similar effect on bureaucracy and red tape. Had it not, you suspect, been for the steady advance of Nazi Germany across continental Europe at the time, then it's quite probable that the MoS would still be the subject of planning meetings and assorted think tanks.

One of the MoS's first post-war responsibilities was that of aircraft production. This included all ongoing research and development relating to air defences, a large and growing file that included the country's atomic weapons programme.

Following the MoS's abolition in 1959, the Ministry of Defence (MoD) was formed in its wake. MoS had, by now, established an Atomic Weapons Research Establishment (AWRE) which was based at the site of the former RAF station at Aldermaston, in Berkshire, an otherwise rather unremarkable little town around 10 miles south-west of Reading.

With its title now clipped to the slightly more punchy AWE (Atomic Weapons Research), the site at Aldermaston shares responsibility for the design, manufacture and supply of warheads for the UK's nuclear weapons.

The site is hardly subtle. How can it be if you call yourself the Atomic Weapons Establishment? No room for doubt there. So, it is hardly shrouded in mystery; a fine covering of radioactive dust, maybe, but certainly no mystery. I haven't tried it myself yet but I suspect that if you give them a ring (and there is a number for their main switchboard freely available as well as, a tad worryingly, one for their seismology department) then I'm sure a cheerful member of white-coated staff will answer with the salutation, 'Good morning, Atomic Weapons Establishment, how can I help you?'

The site at Aldermaston covers around 750 acres and describes itself as a '... centre of excellence, housing advanced research, design and manufacturing facilities', which all sounds rather nice. Except, of course, the items being manufactured, known as Trident, have a thermonuclear warhead which sits atop a missile capable of travelling up to 7,500 miles and, upon reaching its destination, being accurate to within a few feet. Which means that as I write this, one of the UK's nuclear submarines could fire one from its location deep beneath the surface of the Indian Ocean with a more than fair chance that it could, if its captain decreed, fly in through my window before blowing me (and most of Norfolk) to several levels of oblivion.

British engineering, eh? Best in the world.

AWE's remarkably user-friendly website does its best to reassure its visitors that their presence in leafy Berkshire is a vital one, which is a tough sell for any PR guru to make. We can only hope that the science and engineering advances they employ in order to keep, at least in theory, the UK and its allies safe from attack from any rogue foreign power might also, in time, have hither-to unrealised benefits that can help to build worlds rather than destroy them.

Entrance gate to the AWE at Aldermaston. Note the speed limit.

2. Alderney, Channel Islands

Lager Sylt Concentration Camp

There are those who will, if suitably provoked, stand up and declare with pride that Great Britain has not been invaded by an aggressor's armed forces since William the Conqueror came, saw and lived up to his name in 1066.

But they would be wrong.

Because for much of the Second World War, the Channel Islands were occupied by Nazi armed forces; the result of a relatively straight forward invasion by the Wehrmacht, who had initially regarded the option of taking the islands by force with no little caution, assuming, incorrectly as it turned out, that they were heavily armed and defended by elements of both the British Army and Royal Air Force (RAF). This meant that an original plan to take the islands with two battalions of assault troops was unnecessary and, sensing an opportunity to seize the islands and the glory for themselves without the need to risk either men or equipment in great quantities, the islands were eventually taken by a small force from the Luftwaffe. Jersey duly surrendered on 1 July 1940, Alderney a day later with Sark capitulating on 4 July with shipborne German troops landing on the islands for the first time at St Peter Port ten days later.

A small-scale dress rehearsal for the real thing? Maybe. What was hugely important, as far as Nazi Germany was concerned, was the symbolic value of the capturing of the Channel Islands. They'd conquered most of Europe and had now, with little to no resistance, placed boots on the ground on British home soil for the first time.

The Lager Sylt Concentration Camp was built in January 1940 – one of four that were constructed on the Channel Islands at that time. It was not constructed, however, for the forced imprisonment of islanders, but as a base for Russian and other forced labourers to be securely held. That didn't mean, however, that you might be exempt from being sent there if you were a native islander. The initial German approach to the islands and its resident population was to attempt to preserve as much of the 'status quo' as possible (i.e. the islanders would be permitted to carry on living their lives in pretty much the same way they had prior to the invasion). Thus the theatres and cinemas stayed open, while active resistance against the invaders was discouraged because of the very real fears of what might happen if, in the face of armed resistance, the well armed and trained occupying troops carried out reprisal strikes on the local population with, at one point, the islands' Attorney General imploring the British Government to, '… leave the Channel Islands in peace'.

Looking back at this period of history now it comes across as a very benign invasion and occupation. This was not, of course, the case. Lager Sylt's presence on Alderney was a full and very forceful indication of just what Hitler's real intentions were for all of Britain, and that this was just the first outpost where undesirables could be sent to live out whatever was left of their lives. Russian prisoners made up the very great bulk of those held there but, after a while, Lager Sylt became a subcamp of the infamous Neuengamme and its network of satellite concentration camps that were scattered across Northern Germany from 1938 onwards. Over 100,000 prisoners are estimated to have come through that network, Lager Sylt included, with a little under half of that number dying while being held in captivity. The Nazis may well have wanted their occupation of the Channel Islands to look benign, but it was anything but, especially given the fact that it was administered by the SS.

Sylt also held Jewish enforced labourers, captured and sent to the islands to make up the workforce that built many of the military fortifications and installations throughout Alderney. Little remains of the site today other than three gateposts at the rear of the island's airport that mark its original entrance, one of which has a commemorative plaque attached. There are also some modest ruins, including some sentry posts as well as some of the original foundations of the main camp.

If you entered Lager Sylt unwillingly then there was little to no chance of you coming out again. Which makes it one of the most darkly forbidding places in this entire book.

Part of the fortifications near Lager Sylt on Alderney.

3. Barnham, Suffolk

RAF Barnham Nuclear Weapon Storage Site (NSS)

Barnham is one of those typically sleepy East Anglian villages.

It has all the chocolate box accoutrements you could ask for. Mention in Domesday Book? Check. A picturesque village church? Check. Windmill? Check. Quaint nineteenth-century railway station that ended up being butchered by Beeching? Most certainly.

All of that, plus a facility that would have been one of the first on the list for total and utter annihilation had the country been subjected to an all-out nuclear attack by Soviet forces during the Cold War.

Let's be honest. If that had ever happened, then most of East Anglia would have been turned into a fiery wasteland with a population of zero (nil). Barnham would have been one of the key reasons for the region's swift and violent extinction.

That's because RAF Barnham was a high-security storage facility for nuclear weapons, deadly ordnance that was held at the station throughout the fifties and sixties, a fact that, if it was relatively unknown at the time, would certainly have become one more apparent to local residents if the UK had ever been close to nuclear war. That is because that normally very unobtrusive station would, all of a sudden, have become extremely busy with a constant and noisy array of large vehicles arriving and departing on a regular basis, intent on shifting parts of its deadly arsenal to wherever it might have been needed. By now, of course, the local population may well have been in receipt of the Government's jolly handy *Protect and Survive* leaflet which, among other things, advised that the most effective method of protecting oneself from a nuclear blast was to prop a mattress up against an interior wall and snuggle up together behind it with a few bottles of water and a bucket.

Advice which the countries politicians would, of course, be taking heed of themselves as they scampered for the deep and relatively luxurious underground bunkers as far away from the perceived action as their legs (or PA's) could carry them.

One of RAF Barnham's major purposes was to serve the RAF's Vulcan V-Bomber Squadrons and their lethal payloads. These once familiar delta-winged aircraft were unique in that they were able to head far enough east to be able to drop their bombs onto enemy territory in what would have been a one-way trip for its crew, simply because there would almost certainly have been no functioning RAF bases left for them to return to upon the completion of their duties.

Prior to its use as a nuclear depository, RAF Barnham had another deadly purpose, as it had been previously used during the Second World War as a chemical weapon storage facility and filling station, as well as being utilised as a bomb dump for 'conventional' ordnance.

During the years of the Cold War, RAF Barnham would certainly have been a site known to enemy intelligence and, even if it had not been prioritised as a target for a first strike, would almost certainly have been targeted in any second wave of enemy nuclear missiles, the consequence of that meaning, as described above, that much of East Anglia as we know it would have been permanently removed from the map.

There was never any suggestion of RAF Barnham's sinister role in any of the official documentation held at the time when it was simply referred to as a 'Special Storage Site'. This might have implied to people it was where the RAF's supplies of paperclips and staples were kept, so innocuous was the title. Fortunately for both the village and the area itself, the base's role as a nuclear weapon repository ceased in the summer of 1963.

At least that's what they want us to think.

Each of these little storage buildings at RAF Barnham housed a nuclear warhead.

4. Belfast, Counties Antrim & Down

River Farset

The name 'Belfast' is derived From the Irish *Béal Feirste,* which translates as 'the sandy ford at the mouth of the Farset'.

Thus, Belfast is named after this ancient river. Which might be a tad confusing to some as the river that flows through Belfast today is the River Lagen, which ends its 53-mile journey by flowing into the intertidal sea inlet of Belfast Lough.

So, what happened to the River Farset?

Rest assured, it is still very much alive, well and flowing through Belfast. It's just that you can't see very much of it anymore. For, much like the River Fleet, which winds a sinuous route underneath modern London, the River Farset lies buried beneath Belfast's streets, in some cases, as little as just 60 cm (approximately 2 feet) beneath the surface of the modern city. And make no mistake about it, Belfast really does owe not only its origins but its growth and early prosperity to this now hidden and largely forgotten waterway which has, for 170 years, found itself sealed off from the outside world by a network of tunnels.

The city was founded at a natural crossing point where the Farset flowed into the Lagan, forming a narrow sandbar at what is now the corner of Victoria Street and High Street. The site is now occupied by the imposing Victorian church of St George, which stands itself on the site where, around 800 years ago, an ancient chapel welcomed pilgrims who would gather there to pray prior to attempting to cross the two rivers. In time, protestant settlers from both England and Scotland took up a rather more permanent residential status at the site and, by the late eighteenth century, a growing merchant town had sprung from the sand, with the banks of the Farset crammed full of ships moored up to docks and piers of all shapes and sizes. Belfast, from its humble origins, was very much a place on the up. The Farset soon became part of the network of Belfast rivers that was tapped into to provide the raw power needed for the city's textile mills, distilleries and factories – all part of the growing industrial revolution, which was as much a part of life in this part of Great Britain as it was London and all of the great northern cities of England, where it is more commonly celebrated. This is a pity as Belfast was fast becoming an industrial behemoth to rival any of its peers away across the Irish Sea. By the end of the 1800s, the Farset had helped to establish Belfast as one of the leading linen manufacturers in the world, with an estimated 50,000 people working in the mills that were scattered across its banks, leading author Ruairí Ó Baoill to summarise that, '... back then, you probably would have smelled Belfast before you saw it'*.

---

* Ó Baoill, Ruairí, *Hidden History Below Our Feet: The Archaeological Story of Belfast,* (Tandem Design), 2011.

And that was the problem. Because with Belfast's rapid growth to being one of the leading manufacturing cities in Europe, the River Farset had turned from a river into an open sewer; a depository for all manner of human and industrial waste. It was there and it was convenient and, not to put too fine a point on it, if you had something unpleasant or toxic you wanted to get rid of in a hurry, then you threw or tipped it into the Farset and forgot about it. The resultant smell was so bad that in an attempt to hide away the malodorous odours once and for all, the commissioners of Belfast decided to hide it away forever. Thus, by 1848 and after the use of around one million bricks, the River Farset disappeared underneath Belfast and was largely forgotten with its now invisible course giving High Street its distinctive curve, flowing on to the left of the Albert Memorial Clock before, finally, the onlooker gets a fleeting chance to see this ancient river above the ground as it empties into the Lagan at Donegall Quay.

A precious opportunity to glimpse a long-forgotten river that spawned a mighty city.

Named after the lost river that flows into the harbour, the Belfast-based tug *Farset*.

5. Brancaster, Norfolk

MoD ROC Underground Monitoring Post

There are, at a rough estimate, around 1,575 of these facilities scattered throughout Great Britain. The reason I have picked the post at Brancaster, in Norfolk, for this book was that it was a site that held a certain fascination for me as I grew up in the village where this one is situated. The site at Brancaster was, like its 1,574 peers, managed and staffed by volunteer members of the Royal Observer Corp (ROC). This was a civil defence organisation whose core role was to detect, identify, track and report aircraft flying over Great Britain, primarily those who either weren't where they were supposed to be at any given time or, on a rather more sinister level, weren't meant to be there at all.

Nice if you were a plane spotter. But the role of the ROC's volunteers took another step into the dark side towards the end of the 1950s when their personnel were advised that, in the event of a nuclear attack on Britain, they would be expected to seal themselves into their observation posts and provide essential data on the position and magnitude of any atomic weapons that were detonated during the conflict, as well as providing meteorological reports on wind speed and direction, which were used to estimate where and when any radioactive fallout might occur. It all seems, in hindsight, a rather pointless exercise. If Britain had ever been subjected to the full might of the Soviet Union's nuclear arsenal, then you would hardly need a few doughty individuals holed up under the ground to let you know where some of them had gone off. Atomic bombs are not the most subtle of weapons and if one detonates, say, even within 100 miles of where you might happen to be at the time, then you're going to know all about it. But no, for even as the four horsemen of the apocalypse were saddling up their steeds, there would still be a need for reports to be made and paperwork to be filled in. This meant that, if half a dozen or so nuclear detonations took place across East Anglia, boxes had to be ticked and duplicates made. Not even Armageddon can foil bureaucracy. Life in the bunker would have been very uncomfortable for those ROC volunteers who had signed on to carry out the grim work required. First and foremost, they would have had to be prepared, at very short notice, to walk away from their family knowing that it was almost certainly the last time they would have seen them. There would have been many, despite all of their best intentions, who would not have been able to do this and, subsequently, would simply not have turned up for duty. For those that did, initial contact would either have been made by telephone or by a knock on the door; a designated 'team leader', having been advised directly, would have called in to pick them up by car. No questions asked, no formal goodbyes, just a hurried and unannounced departure.

The bunker would have been well stocked with supplies. The MoD used a shop in nearby Hunstanton for the facility in Brancaster as the shop owner would also have been a volunteer. Most of the supplies provided would have been items that would have lasted for a long time (e.g. tinned food and preserves) and could have been stored away easily. Other items would either have been bought fortnightly (e.g. biscuits), while perishables such as bread and milk would have been topped up on a weekly basis with the overall objective being that there were enough supplies provided to sustain the team of volunteers for at least three, maybe four weeks. At the very top of the entrance tunnel was a raised plinth that was reached by climbing up a few concrete steps. This served as a vantage point for a clear view northward towards the coast which was just over a mile away. Leaving the bunker in order carry out all of their readings and observations would, ultimately, have exposed the volunteers to the radioactive fallout that they were there to report on, meaning that, ultimately, they would have died in the course of their duties. A grim reality of this was the fact that if one of them was dangerously and obviously exposed, it is probable that his or her colleagues would have refused them re-entry into the relatively (as its air was unfiltered and radioactive material would, eventually, have made its way in) safe and sealed world of the bunker.

A truly remarkable and very courageous group of people whose training was, ultimately, never required to be put into serious action.

The entrance to the ROC Observation post at Brancaster.

Right: Inside the ROC observation post at Brancaster.

Below: Note the air filter near to the ROC entry point at Brancaster

6. Burghfield, Berkshire

Atomic Weapons Establishment (AWE)

Connected at the hip with the much more well-known Atomic Weapons Establishment Aldermaston (see 1), AWE Burghfield is a 225-acre site that is, according to the AWE website (and let's face it, if they say so, then it must be true), where '... warheads are assembled and maintained while in service, and decommissioned when out of service'.

How, I wonder, do you decommission a nuclear warhead? Are they delivered to the sites front gate by a man with a clipboard who says, 'fourteen out of date nuclear warheads, sign here please'?

Let's hope that, if that is the case, he goes to the correct address and doesn't end up dropping them somewhere else? And what if HM Government have sourced those deliveries to one of the many courier firms that litter our highways and byways these days; their drivers are hardly the most reliable of people. What if someone gets home from work late on a Tuesday evening to discover fourteen nuclear warheads propped up against their front door with an accompanying note that states, 'We tried to deliver your package today, but you were out'.

'Did you order fourteen nuclear warheads darling?' Shudder!

Burghfield itself is a pleasant village that is popular with commuters, such are its decent links to larger centres of population such as Reading and Basingstoke, via the nearby M4. Its military significance was first made apparent when, in the early years of the Second World War, several wartime facilities and accompanying anti-invasion structures were constructed throughout the area, including a Royal Ordnance Filling Factory (ROF) that went into full production in 1942. These were, as the name suggests, locations where bombs and other forms of ordnance were made, so hardly the safest place for anyone to work or even live near. It was with that latter thought in mind that Burghfield like all the other ROF factories were built in areas that were considered 'relatively safe', which meant, at the time, westward of a line that ran from Weston-super-Mare, in Somerset, towards Haltwhistle, in Northumberland.

Reassuring in some small way, I expect, if you lived in those areas, especially compared to the Midlands and Birmingham, which were considered 'unsafe', while East Anglia and South/South East England were classified as 'dangerous', while your living in or around London was not really a very good thing at all, especially if you lived within exploding distance of the well known ROF at Arsenal (hence the football clubs name) in North London. Burghfield's ROF saw extensive reconstruction work in 1953 but rather than, as the locals might have hoped, it being turned into a nice new school or hospital, the new factory was designed and built with the construction, servicing and decommissioning of missiles in mind.

Missiles that were becoming bigger, noisier, and a lot, LOT more dangerous to be near. And thus, it remains today.

It's still a relatively secret place, of course. We all know it's there and we all think we know what goes on behind its fences and heavily staffed gates. You can't (trust me) just turn up and wander inside for a casual look around, so don't try it. Interestingly, however, AWE Burghfield does attempt, for a 'forbidden' place, to be as open as possible and, to that end, can even be rated on Google. I had a look at some of the comments that had been left on the site with my favourite one saying it all.

'Lots of science'.

Couldn't have put it better myself.

Entrance to the AWE at Burghfield.

7. Caerwent, Monmouthshire

Royal Navy Propellant Factory

You may not have been to, or even heard of Caerwent, which would be a pity as it would be a most agreeable calling off point on any pootle around this part of southern Wales, close enough to Chepstow and its castle as well as everything that the resurgent city of Newport has to offer. Caerwent itself has Roman origins which are nicely shown off by some of the best-preserved Roman ruins in Europe, so definitely somewhere you might want to tarry a while. You might suspect, however, that the powers that be rather hoped that Caerwent remained both out of sight and very definitely out of mind for the casual observer during the Second World War. Because it was chosen as the site for a Royal Navy propellant factory in 1939, that is, a facility where explosives were manufactured and stored along with a variety of munitions, all of which, naturally, could demonstrate their own explosive qualities if duly agitated.

The 'big bang' was, according to modern science, the starting point for everything that exists in the current universe. The big bang that would have occurred at Caerwent had the site been compromised at any time during its peak storage years may not have been that far behind the daddy of them all in terms of size, scale and sound. Yet Caerwent was, reassuringly (except, perhaps for the locals) chosen as the location for this facility because, in terms of both security and safety, it ticked a lot of bureaucratic boxes. It was, for example, perceived to be relatively invulnerable and not likely to be the focus of any aerial attack by aggressive forces (meaning, of course, the Luftwaffe). I have to say that, had I been presented with this 'evidence' at the time, I might just have pointed out the nearby Roman ruins to the brown suits who'd come up from London for the day and mention that, as a Roman army had invaded on the hoof (and that would have been mostly made up of foreign mercenaries – the Roman generals never saw fit to 'waste' their elite forces on out of the way Empire outposts) then shouldn't it been considered possible that the German air force, at that time the best trained and equipped in the world, might have had little to no problem in locating and knocking seven bells out of Caerwent, should they choose?

Caerwent was also away from industrial areas that might have been subjected to attack but was, at the same time, sufficiently close to urban areas from which a large workforce could be drawn. It was also convenient for both the main roads in the area as well as the railways and was nearby to a suitable water supply that could be tapped into as part of the manufacturing process. It was estimated, for example, that to produce 150 tons of cordite per week, the factory would need to make use of 3 million gallons of water per day. So, it was a big site. One that couldn't have been missed from the air by any vigilant spotter. Put it this way, you'd be able to easily tell something was being constructed in Caerwent that wasn't a new village hall or cricket pitch. The total area covered was 1,580 acres, of which 1,163 acres were enclosed by a very stark and obvious factory fence that said, nay shouted for the attention of, again, the casual bystander or lone pilot. Subtle it most certainly wasn't. Secret it most certainly was. It wouldn't have been a particularly nice place to work either. Maybe not too bad if you worked in the main office block but decidedly unpleasant if you were part of the team in the sulphuric acid factory, the acid being used for the manufacture of, among other things, nitro-glycerine – a substance that likes to go 'bang' like few others. This part of the plant was operational twenty-four hours a day, seven days a week. A peek inside its walls at that time must, surely, been like gazing into a Van Eyck vision of hell.

The facility thrived. In the post-war years it produced the Gosling solid rocket booster for Seaslug, the Royal Navy's surface to air missile. It ended up being so successful and productive a site that it caught the eye of the US military, who took over the site in the late 1960s declaring it to be part of the US Army's weapons storage facilities for Europe; a convenient repository for US forces if the Soviet Union had invaded western Europe from the east, providing, of course, said forces hadn't paid a little bit of attention to Caerwent prior to doing so. Fortunately, it was never needed and after the scaling down of the Cold War in the early 1990s the site was closed. It is now used as a military training area and a facility where surplus rail locomotives are either stored or scrapped.

Caerwent – a picturesque village with a sinister neighbour.

8. Cheltenham, Gloucestershire

Government Communications Headquarters (GCHQ)

Have you ever seen an unmarked van parked up near your home for days on end for no apparent reason?

Or why, even on the hottest summer days, a woman in a long coat has repeatedly been sat on the same bench in your local park reading the same copy of the *Daily Telegraph*? Well now you know. It's GCHQ at work.

Not really, of course. The good folk of Government Communications Head Quarters are a lot more subtle than that these days. GCHQ claim to be the world leading intelligence, cyber and security agency. Now, I'm pretty certain that the FBI and Mossad, among others, would like to think that they are actually the holders of that particular title, but short of holding a World Intelligence Agencies World Cup (which would have to be played in secret locations in empty stadiums) we'll never know whose spooks really are the best, so for the sake of good old fashioned patriotism let's assume it is GCHQ. Besides, you never know, they might be monitoring my PC as I am writing this (NO WE'RE NOT-GCHQ) so best to keep them onside.

In an increasingly troubled world, GCHQ do have their work cut out. For want of a better word their mission statement is to 'Keep Britain Safe'. In essence, therefore, they are the country's official caretakers, responsible for the safety and wellbeing of around 67,000,000 people spread out over a surface area of a little less than 81,000 square miles. So, an onerous task however you look at it. The hub of all their hard work is a building referred to colloquially as 'The Doughnut', which is situated on a 176-acre site on the outskirts of the genteel Gloucestershire town of Cheltenham. The Doughnut is the second home to 5,500 employees and is, not surprisingly, the largest single employer in the whole of Gloucestershire. You'd think, therefore, that such a large and mightily impressive building (it would not look out of place in a *Star Wars* film) would have been subject to the most rigorous and exacting design standards but, alas, this was not always the case. Completed in 2004, it was soon found that it was, infact, too small to easily accommodate all of GCHQ's employees, which necessitated the construction of a second building in the local area in order to squeeze them all in. The now wholly completed complex is believed to be the largest building constructed for the means of secret intelligence operations outside of the United States, a mightily impressive boast for a county that is perhaps more well known for a breed of pig and a cheese that is so good its referred to as 'double' Gloucester.

The staff who work there are an eclectic mix of Project Managers, Linguists, Mathematicians and Cryptographers as you will find anywhere in the world. And that's just the tip of a very boffin-rich iceberg. Just imagine the topics of conversation around the water cooler on a typical Monday morning at GCHQ: while the rest of the country will be debating the weekend's TV offerings or the football results, any similar huddle in

The Doughnut, GCHQ, Cheltenham by Ian S - geograph.org.uk/p/2725788

GCHQ's 'doughnut'. Or is it a spaceship?

The Doughnut will centre on algorithms, orismology, FORTRAN and how the Cherry and White's got on at the weekend.

But not everyone at GCHQ is a hugely intelligent person in a white coat. The strength of the organisation is the great variety of people it employs and the personal and professional strengths that they bring to the table. So yes, while there may be a greater than average smattering of PhDs dotted about the place, there will also be an army of administrators doing their own jobs to the very best of their abilities in order that those who are there 24/7 and 365 days a year, utilising their mighty brains in order to keep us all safe (and let the likes of me write this sort of nonsense about them), are able to do that.

But if you ask me, it looks nothing like a doughnut. Because it's really a spaceship.

9. City of London, London

Bank of England Gold Vault

It's usually considered sensible to keep quiet about any valuable items that you might happen to have in your home.

You wouldn't, after all, go into a crowded bar and loudly announce to all and sundry who you were and where you lived before adding that you had a genuine Canaletto hanging in your downstairs loo. Because if you did, then it's quite likely that someone would have nicked it before you'd finished your half of lager.

It's different if you're the Bank of England. They've got hard cash to spare and they don't care who knows it. You only have to visit their website and there it is emblazoned across the PC monitors, laptops, tablets and mobile devices of the world for all to see, the financial equivalent of 'My Dad is bigger than your Dad'.

The Bank of England has one of the world's largest gold vaults. We are the second largest custodian of gold in the world, after the New York Federal Reserve.

All written against a backdrop of large piles of gold bars, all stacked up on sets of those blue shelving units you might be familiar with if you have the tyres on your car changed as one of those 'While You Wait' places. Except these aren't radials and remoulds, they're gold ingots; thousands of them. Around 6,000 tonnes of the stuff in total that covers an area of 300,000 square feet, and worth, in total, approximately £172 billion. That's 172, followed by twelve, yes twelve, zeros. So, a lot of money. Put it another way, enough for (at the time of writing) every man, woman and child on the face of the earth to be given £12,919.31, give or take a few pence either way. So, there's a LOT of money down there. The Bank of England makes this claim knowing that there is absolutely no chance of you, I or any of the fictional cast of the *Ocean's Eleven* film breaking into their vault and making off with them in the back of a van. Because it's just about the most secure money depository in the world. And that includes Fort Knox which, as everyone knows, was wiped clean of its gold by the aptly named Goldfinger in the James Bond film of the same name.

He wouldn't have got away with it here. Because not only are the walls that line the vault said to be 8-foot thick, the keys needed to get into the vaults (which are actually used for purely ceremonial purposes, not that anyone is going to be invited to come and watch any time soon) are more than a foot long with the locks now incorporating voice-operated software. And here's another thing. They could probably fit all of the gold down there into a slightly smaller vault, but because the bedrock that the Bank of England is built upon is London Clay (which tends to be a bit squishy), the gold bars can only be stacked to a height of four pallets in the top level of the vaults, and six levels high in the bottom ones. If they stacked them any higher, they'd start to sink into the ground.

That's not to say that the Bank of England's vaults have never been breached. The official line, at least, is that in their 325-year-long history no unauthorised entry has ever been successfully made. However, one tale tells of a nineteenth-century Victorian sewer worker who did manage to find himself in the vaults after a little bit of judicious study (and a lot of wriggling). He was, it is said, honest enough to have not helped himself to even one bar of gold during his excursions into the vault, a fact that the bank's relieved (and mightily embarrassed) directors acknowledged by rewarding him with the not inconsiderable sum of £800.

Thus proving that, in this case, grime did pay.

The Bank of England. About as close to the vaults as you're likely to get.

10. City of Westminster, London

Queen's Private Rooms, Buckingham Palace

Have you been inside Buckingham Palace? I have. It's not to my taste. The carpets are far too loud for one thing, while it's also one of the last buildings in London that utilises wallpaper rather than a nice coat of emulsion. And all that artwork crammed onto every spare piece of space (I guess there is one advantage to that, all those Van Dyck's and Bellini's do, at least, hide the wallpaper) on the walls, there's no room for a nice bookcase anywhere. You can tell so much about people by browsing through their collection of books. Plus, if your bookcase includes any of my books, I will like you very much.

I bet the Queen doesn't much like the decor either. She comes across as the sensible type who would normally eschew vulgarity of any kind for common sense and practicality. So, while she might not particularly like walking down long corridors that contain all the colours of the rainbow, she can at least comfort herself by knowing that those parts of her not particularly loved London home look that way to keep the likes of us happy. No, she much prefers the sanctuary of her own living space within the Palace which reflects her character a lot more.

The Palace was built by the Duke of Buckingham in 1703, before eventually falling into the hands of King George III six decades later. It largely remained unaltered until a spectacularly lavish refurbishment began in the nineteenth century. The Palace contains a total of 775 rooms (including 188 staff bedrooms, ninety-two offices and seventy-eight bathrooms), while the Queen's own apartment contains just nine rooms; a fairly modest number when you consider that even the average semi-detached house today will consist of at least five rooms and usually more. She does, however, have what is known as the 'Queen's Audience Room' within her apartments, one where she not only hosts members of her household but also, on a weekly basis, whoever her Prime Minister happens to be at the time. The room is decorated in a far less ostentatious style than much of the Palace, featuring pale blue walls and dark wooden flooring with an array of framed family photographs arranged on the furniture, giving it a cosy and much more family friendly look than some of the formal rooms within the Palace.

Buckingham Palace usually 'has the builders in' as plans to upgrade its plumbing, electrics and other parts of the Palace which are, shall we say, starting to show their age, are made fit for purpose for at least another fifty years. So the work is ongoing. This has caused, as you would expect (or be more than familiar with), some disruption in the day to day activities in and around the Palace, as the team of builders charged with doing the work exchange sharp intakes of breath and collectively tut at the state of the cornicing in the ballroom. One of the tasks that will take place while the work is being done (completion is expected in or around the year 2026) is replacing 100 miles of electrical cabling that was first installed in the 1950s and doing the same with 1,250 light fittings in the South Wing.

According to some reports one builder when asked the timeless question of whether or not he would like a cup of tea replied to the affirmative, adding that it had to be 'builder's tea' (i.e. strong and sweet enough for the teaspoon to stand up in). He was more than surprised, when upon looking up after the tea was brought to him, that it had been made and delivered by HRH herself who had, you would think, purloined a couple of teabags from her own private supply in order to make it. Numerous stories about the Queen's kitchen and her eating preferences have been leaked to the press over the years, including the fact that she particularly likes Special K breakfast cereal, enjoys Darjeeling tea (although I suspect it wasn't Darjeeling that she served to the builder) and insists on much of her food being stored in Tupperware containers.

Buckingham Palace. Which window is HRH's?

11. Clydach Gorge, Abergavenny

Ogof Craig A Ffynnon Caves

I love the beautifully understated snippets of information contained deep within one of the websites dedicated to this spectacular system of caves in South Wales.

'A large quantity of rock has fallen from the rock face above the entrance' it intones, before warning that, '… there is still more rock that is likely to fall'. But that's not all. If you managed to avoid a 40-ton rock falling on your head, then do pay particular heed to the advice that follows, the one that mentions that the picturesquely named 'Gasoline Alley' (I thought all caves had beguiling names like 'Blue Grotto' and 'Cave of the Crystals'?) 'floods to the roof following heavy rain'.

It's not the sort of information that's going to make me want to see what life as a Morlock was like in any particular hurry. Yet, just to make absolutely sure that they've successfully weeding out the wimps at the earliest possible opportunity, the narrative draws to a close with chilling dose of reality.

'Caving…', the website concludes, '…can be a dangerous activity'.

I used to work with a dedicated caver. He'd graft away from Monday to Friday before, at weekends, driving off to one of the more remote parts of the country to find the deepest, darkest and dankest hole in the ground before flinging himself into it for a couple of days or so. He especially enjoyed, as I recall, having to squeeze through particularly narrow passages, places that, if you weren't careful, you could end up being stuck in. He reckoned being in such a potentially perilous situation really 'focuses the mind'. I bet it does. And I'll add to that by saying that if it was me in that sort of situation, it wouldn't as much focus my mind as freely and spectacularly relax my sphincter muscle.

Ogof Craig A Ffynnon is not a cave for tourists. Put it this way, having a leisurely stroll into Wookey Hole in Somerset does not, in anyway, prepare you for this subterranean behemoth.

The cave is around 4 miles in length and is regarded as one of the more visually appealing in Wales. Much (I suspect) to the delight of the seasoned caver, it contains an early abundance of sections where your only method of forward locomotion would involve crawling on all fours, part of that section being in a part of the cave that is regarded as 'arduous and uncomfortable'. This precedes some extremely wet and muddy passages before opening out and into a cathedral-like space known as the 'Hall of the Mountain King', a large and welcome open cavern that contains an abundance of flowstones which, for those that want to know more, are made up of sheet-like deposits of calcite and other minerals which are formed as water flows through the floor of a cave. After duly admiring all of this, the intrepid caver has to move on into what follows the Hall of the Mountain King, which is a long series of low passages where, no doubt, plenty of minds have been focused as generation after generation of caver has squeezed and cajoled their complaining bodies through ever narrowing gaps, which sounds great fun.

An intrepid explorer enters the cave network at Ogof Craig A Ffynnon.

For the seasoned caver, a trip here will be regarded as a fairly strenuous, but by no means impossible, day out doing what they love to do. For the rest of us however, conditioned both throughout life and in both literature and legend, venturing into the bowels of the earth is something that, with the best will in the world, you really want to avoid if at all possible. It still serves to remind us that in our ever more sanitised and safety conscious world there are still plenty of opportunities to take risks and stare potential danger in the face, however forbidding the environment might be.

---

*   http://www.ogof.org.uk/ogof-craig-a-ffynnon.html

12. Coastal Waters, Suffolk

Principality of Sealand

Sealand, based on the old military fortress of Roughs Tower off the East Anglian coast, lays claim to be the 'smallest country in the world' by virtue of its claim to have been an independent sovereign state since 1967. It all makes for a good story but, sadly for Sealand and all who live atop her, she is not officially recognised by any other sovereign state, with the United Nations (UN) having a final say by stating that, 'artificial islands, installations and structures do not possess the status of islands.' The spoilsports.

Nice try Sealand, admirable even. But you remain a bastion of impossible romance 8 miles off the Suffolk coast and therefore remain English and part of England. But what a remarkable story you have to tell.

Sealand is, in reality, an example of what are known as Maunsell Forts and was then known as Roughs Tower. These were built in the Thames and Mersey estuaries during the Second World War in order to help defend those parts of the British coast from attacks by enemy shipping, and were manned by personnel from either the Army or, as was the case for Roughs Tower, men from the Royal Navy, who stationed there until 1956 when it was decommissioned. Roughs Tower then lived a lonely and fairly quiet life until 1965 when it was occupied by staff from the pirate station *Wonderful Radio London*. Two years later those broadcasters were removed from Roughs Tower by a former Army Major, Roy Bates, who intended to use the old fortress as a base for his own pirate station which he had called, very imaginatively, *Radio Essex*.

With pirate radio being very much in vogue at the time (the most famous, *Radio Caroline*, was launched in 1964) his actions caused a minor ripple on the waters but were soon forgotten. Bates, however, had bigger and better ideas for Roughs Tower and rather than commencing broadcasting from there he declared that Roughs Tower was now independent and had been renamed the Principality of Sealand. He took his new role as leader of the world's newest country rather seriously. For example, in 1968, when a group of workmen arrived to service a vital navigational buoy that was situated near to Roughs Tower, Michael Bates, Roy Bates' son, attempted to warn them off by firing warning shots in their direction from the tower. Being a British subject, he was duly summoned to court in England to answer firearm charges but had all the answers, getting the case dismissed as Roughs Tower was situated outside of British territorial waters.

Bates held firm and in 1975 introduced an official constitution for Sealand, as well as a national flag, anthem and passports. Sealand has also minted its own currency and printed its own stamps. It is, in short, everything a country should be and has everything you would expect one to have. The only problem is that over five decades since Roy Bates (who died in 2012) made the rest of the world aware of his dream, that very same world still refuses to recognise it.

While Sealand is not, strictly speaking, a 'forbidden' territory in the truest sense of the word, visits to the principality are very much discouraged and it is likely that anyone who fancies sailing over for a chat and a cup of tea would be met with a lack of cooperation and a refusal to let them land. The current advice being issued from Sealand is that visits are not normally permitted with 'the current international situation and other factors' being cited as the reason behind this policy. Applications for visas are therefore not being accepted at the time of writing.

So, you're less likely to get offered a guided tour of Sealand than you are one of the Atomic Weapons Establishment. Sealand does, however, have its own honours system and, for the bargain price of just £499.99 (at the time of writing) you can become a Duke or Duchess of the Principality of Sealand and, with it, probably increase your chances of receiving an invitation to visit the world's most unusual non-country.

Money talks in even this brave new world.

Sealand proudly flying its flag, in spite of not being recognised – anywhere – as an independent country.

13. Cobham, Surrey

Chelsea FC Training Ground

I'm a football fan. Guilty as charged. I've even written books about my favourite football team and have ghostwritten a couple of autobiographies for two of their more well-known players. Yet, for all that, there is no doubt in my mind whatsoever that I no longer enjoy the modern game as much as I did even five years ago. It has become a slave to money. Big money. Obscene, filthy, immoral and eyebrow raising amounts of money. It won't be long, I believe, until the modern game sinks in the financial morass it has begat for itself. And maybe when, rather than if, that happens it will come as a blessing and see the game reborn and re-energised without the tainted stain of the green. A particularly common gripe among today's average football supporter is how removed from reality the players have become. These are not, lest we forget, people who excel at science, technology, medicine, music, education, government, literature or anyone of 101 plus admirable practical skills and qualities. The elite clubs hardly help matters. They pander to the egos of their star players in the way a doting parent mollycoddles a starstruck five-year-old at a beauty pageant. Star performers are protected from prying eyes, cameras and pencils at all times, whether that be before or after a game or even when they come into work every morning. Take, for example, Chelsea FC's training ground at Cobham, in Surrey. It wasn't so long ago that professional footballers could frequently be seen being put through their paces at a local public recreation ground or school playing field. Or, if the club was based anywhere near the coast, running along the beach in true *Chariots of Fire* style. They were a familiar sight, so much so that the public pretty much ignored them and let them get on with their work. No-one, after all, felt like popping into the nearest factory or shop to talk to and gawk at the people hard at work there, so why do the same with a bunch of footballers? No, let them get on with their work and save the public adulation/dissection for 90 minutes or so from 3 p.m. on a Saturday afternoon.

Until 2005, Chelsea used to train at a facility owned by Imperial College London. It was based at Harlington in-between the M4 and Heathrow Airport and was shared with the students. So it wasn't unknown for one of the clubs stars to discover his clothes had been moved outside the changing rooms by a student when he overstayed his welcome at the facility one afternoon. Whether you were a student or an international footballer, the same rules applied to everyone and this was, and still is, right. But all that changed when the big money came to Chelsea. Players and staff were soon spirited away from Harlington to a new multi-million-pound training ground at Cobham in leafy Surrey. It includes first class gym and medical facilities, as well as hydrotherapy facilities and an underwater treadmill. And no, I didn't realise there was even such a thing until I researched this piece. But there you go, Chelsea have one and, what's more, it has depth and incline controls as well as a video monitoring option. Marvellous. The whole site is spread over 140 acres, an area that includes over thirty pitches. Most are, given how treacherously icy a typical

Surrey winter can be, replete with undersoil heating systems. Nice for the players I guess but at what cost to the environment? In addition to providing all of this and more to their senior players, Cobham is also the home of the club's junior sides; 150 young players who are looked after by over seventy full-time staff in state of the art classrooms on site. It is, in essence, a state-of-the-art sporting, medical and educational facility that is as good as any in the whole of Europe.

Chelsea have, to their credit, made attempts to share the site with other sporting organisations. But even that smacks a little bit of elitism. An amateur club, for example, play their home matches on one of the sites pitches, but even they are made up of the 'old boys' from Malvern College in Worcestershire, which is around 150 miles away. So hardly a gesture that benefits the local community. It might be nice, for example, if they allowed a pub team from, say Woking, Staines or Leatherhead to play there, a much more realistic gesture to share their site with people from a community that make up much of the club's support.

Such a shame that 'the people's game' doesn't seem to be about and for the people anymore. Football clubs used to be the very heart and soul of a community. Now they are anything but, hiding themselves away, as Chelsea have done, behind high walls, spotlights and security patrols. Forbidden football at its most exclusive.

As close as you can get to Chelsea's training ground (left of photo) near Cobham, in Surrey.

14. Faslane, Helensburgh

UK Nuclear Submarine Base

If, like me, you are a dedicated user of the nation's railway network, you may have noted that many station signs on their respective concourses pay homage to the town or city they are situated in. Vauxhall in London cites that it is home to the Oval Cricket Ground for example, while upon arriving at Aberdour you will be informed that you need to alight here for the Fife Coastal Path. In more recent years, rather sadly, the bean counters at National Rail soon realised that this otherwise informative and old-fashioned way of linking a station with a nearby attraction might make them a little bit of money, poor underfunded paupers that they are. Thus the whole scheme was opened up to commercial exploitation, the result of which sees travellers to Newbury being advised that they have arrived at the home of a telecommunications business while, if you are getting off your train at Queens Road Peckham, prepare to be advised that, rather than alighting at an ancient settlement that appears in the Doomsday Book or one of the first places in the world to introduce bus stops and a bus timetable, you are in fact at the home of a property company.

Which isn't terribly exciting is it?

On the other hand, just imagine the potential if, as you rattled your way into Helensburgh station, you were greeted by signage that announced that you had arrived at 'The Home of Britain's Nuclear Submarine Fleet'. The whole place would soon, I am sure, be full of shady looking individuals in Gabardine mackintoshes who'd approach you and say things like 'the shaggy bird has flown the nest' and 'as the pale moon waxes, the dragon holds its breath'. Now that would be exciting. But I'm not sure that the Ministry of Defence would be terribly keen.

Her Majesty's Naval Base Clyde is one of three operating bases in Great Britain for the Royal Navy, the other two being at Devonport and Portsmouth. Clyde, which is based at Faslane, is best known, as my suggestion indicates, for being the home of Britain's nuclear weapons, based here in the form of Trident missiles homed on nuclear powered submarines. It was initially constructed and put into operational use as a Naval base during the Second World War when it was used as a vast marshalling yard (an aquatic storage area where ships and submarines were quartered) before, at the end of that conflict, being used as a place where decommissioned ships could be dismantled, one of these being HMS *Vanguard*, which was the last battleship to be scrapped in Britain. Its purpose was changed when, in the 1960s, Britain entered into talks with the United States regarding the purchase of the then-Naval nuclear deterrent, which was known as Polaris. These negotiations were successful and four nuclear submarines were constructed so that Polaris could be utilised from at least one of them at any given time and date from any place at sea. These submarines would call Faslane their home although, such is the nature of having an active nuclear deterrent, there would always be at least one of them at sea, somewhere, armed and ready to dispatch its deadly payload if the need arose. Faslane's use as the base for these and future vessels of that nature was primarily geographical. The area of water where it is situated is relatively secluded but is deep and fairly easy to navigate. It also allows for a swift dispatch of submarines into the patrolling areas of the North Atlantic as and when required, as well as being conveniently close to the US base at Holy Loch which was operational from 1961 through to 1992. It is interesting, in closing, to speculate on what might happen at Faslane if, at any point in the next couple of decades or so, Scotland successfully declares itself independent of Great Britain and, in such circumstances, it is fair to suggest, perhaps, that a newly formed Scottish administration would request the submarines be relocated from their independent waters as swiftly as possible.

One of Britain's nuclear submarines, with an escort, heads for Faslane and home.

15. Fleet, Dorset

MoD Control Site-Microbiological Research Establishment (MRE)

The curious among us will always want to visit locations where exceedingly unpleasant things have taken place. You can, for example, book a day trip to Chernobyl (would you really want to stay there for any longer?), a tourist destination where, according to one website that is currently promoting 'the most famous Ukrainian phenomenon', you will find, among many other things that, '…radiation makes the zone particularly interesting'.

'Interesting'. I'm sure that the thousands of people who have either died or are currently dying as a result of the world's most infamous nuclear accident found the proliferation of deadly radiation in and around them, their families and homes anything but that.

Great Britain has not, yet, had its own Chernobyl. Yet, regardless of that, there are places in this country where you might just think twice about paying a visit, however curious you might happen to be. Except that, at any given time, thousands of unsuspecting visitors will be all too close to this particular location. The place in question is close to Fleet in Dorset which was where the site used in what was referred to as the Dorset Defence Trials. These were carried out in the 1960s and 1970s, experiments that saw the airborne release of zinc cadmium sulphide over residential areas to simulate what might happen in the event of a genuine chemical attack on this country. The MoD stressed, of course, that the chemicals used were 'harmless' but, given that some families in the area went on to have children with birth defects, there have been calls for an official enquiry. There seemed to be little to no effort made to conceal the experiments as, in another trial using the same chemical compound, a generator was towed along a road close to Frome (population approximately 26,000) that generously emitted the chemical into the air for at least an hour. These experiments were not just restricted to the West Country either as, in early 1964, it was reported that the MoD had carried out germ warfare aerial spraying over Norwich for much the same reasons: to simulate such an attack and to assess, from that, how the airborne particles might have behaved, given the meteorological conditions at the time. This programme was regarded as 'Top Secret' until 2000, when it was eventually declassified.

A report was duly commissioned and written called *The Fluorescent Particle Trials* (sounds gripping) which revealed how, from 1955 through to 1963, aircraft flew from the north east of England down to the tip of Cornwall, ejecting, en route, huge amounts of the aforementioned zinc cadmium sulphide onto an unsuspecting population. Experiments of a similar nature were also carried out in London during the mid-1950s when bacteria was released on the London Underground between Colliers Wood and Tooting Broadway. Nowhere and no-one, it seemed, was safe from potentially being poisoned via the actions of their own government. The site near to Fleet was also near to seaborne trials that took place off that part of the Dorset coast involving the vessels *Night Ferry* and *Golden Arrow*

The Dorset coast near Fleet. It all looks so tranquil…

Frome, in Somerset, used for chemical weapons trials in the 1950s.

(the Government have long learnt that if you want to utilise something or somewhere that is potentially harmful to the public, give it a really pleasant and fluffy name like, for example, Sellafield, which sounds so much more unthreatening than Windscale), which were used to oversee the airborne experiments.

These accounts, and others, featured in an online article in the *Guardian* that concluded with the writer of the piece enquiring of a spokeswoman from the Porton Down 'science park' if the sort of experiments that had centered on Fleet and the surrounding areas were still being carried out. Her response was, to say the least, a telling one.

'It is not our policy to discuss ongoing research'.

I'll leave you to draw your own conclusions. But I wouldn't be 100 per cent happy about eating any fruit or vegetables that might have been grown in that otherwise rich and fertile Dorset soil.

16. Foulness Island, Essex

MoD Weapons Testing Centre

The East Anglian coast is a beautiful part of the country. Unspoilt sandy beaches, big skies, infinite networks of creeks stretching out and over seemingly endless tracts of salt marsh. It is categorically not, as Amanda insists in Noel Coward's *Private Lives*, 'flat' but it does have a undulating beauty about it that is utterly captivating. Norfolk (the focus of Amanda's ignorant derision) and Suffolk steal the hearts and headlines for the most part, yet Essex has its fair share of beguiling beaches – Thorpe Bay, Martello Beach and Walton-on-the-Naze, to name but three.

And then there is Foulness Island. It's one of those places that you may well have heard of but are not quite sure why. It sits a little over 10 miles to the north-east of the cheeky hustle and bustle of Southend-on-Sea, a few thousand acres of rambler friendly marshland, a destination that should, even in this bird rich part of the country, be an absolute mecca for twitchers and dog walkers alike. Yet for all of that, it's not a place where casual visits are encouraged or even, at times, welcomed. Indeed, it's one that the MoD would rather (in the same way the USAF regards Area 51) you never knew was there at all. They've long used it as their veritable playground for testing a whole array of weapons such as rockets, missiles (surface to air or anti-tank, Sir?) grenades and other instruments of death including, in all likelihood, things we don't even think have been invented yet. Which, of course, is why they'd rather we all kept away from the place.

The trouble with that is the island is home to around 150 residents who, despite the MoD's best efforts, aren't that keen on leaving the place and are continuing to rent their homes and farms from their military landlords. They'll be more than familiar with the island and the idiosyncrasies of life there but not so the casual traveller. The approach to Foulness from nearby Great Wakering involves myriad red danger signs, forbidding barbed wire fences and a security checkpoint before you join a military road that takes you over a bridge and onto the island itself. Luckily for both parties they seem, for the most part, to get on with one another. They have had, after all, many years of practice. It's folk like you and me, outsiders (and, as far as the MoD is concerned, potential spies) that have to keep our wits about us.

If you're lucky enough to arrive on the island unimpeded by men with guns, you'll begin to notice that things are beginning to get a bit scary. For instead of all the normal accoutrements of the seaside, you will now find yourself confronted by old air raid shelters, weirdly shaped buildings, some of which are topped with satellite dishes, and numerous old warehouses, all of which look like they might – they just might – have been the secret hideaway for a flying saucer at some point in the past. At this point, you wouldn't be blamed for wanting to take your windbreak and egg mayonnaise sandwiches somewhere else.

Public access to Foulness is restricted although members of the public are welcome to visit the island by means of a formal invitation. However, even this glimmer of light is partially dulled by a warning that persons accessing the island who are not familiar with it might quite easily find themselves in trouble, due to the strong and unpredictable (presumably one of the reasons the MoD are there?) tidal flows that surround the island. And that's before you even take into consideration stumbling across something that is covered by the Official Secrets Act.

So yes, you can visit Foulness Island if you really – really – want to. But be prepared to be treated like a visiting aunt or uncle at Christmas if you do, in that everyone will make you feel more than welcome but they'll hide all the good food and drink from you and, in reality, don't want you there at all and can't wait for you to leave.

Approaching Foulness Island.

17. Glen Douglas, Argyll and Bute

Military Munitions Depot

Let's be honest. For all of our so called 'special relationship' with the United States, it does tend to be one where the bigger and more powerful of the two nations takes advantage of the situation wherever and whenever they can; especially when it comes to facilities, military or otherwise, that might be first, second and third on any potential aggressors wish list. Where, for example, did the United States Air Force choose to deploy many of its cruise missiles during the Cold War? At RAF Greenham Common and RAF Molesworth. Then there was the attack made by US aircraft on Libya in 1986, one that, according to reports at the time, caused forty deaths, many of whom were civilians. Those raids were launched from RAF Lakenheath and RAF Upper Heyford, an act of aggression that was later condemned by the United Nations General Assembly who considered it 'a violation of the Charter of the United Nations and of international law'. Even today, US nuclear weapons are still stationed and maintained at bases in Great Britain, a situation which, as recently as 2019, led to leading Russian senator Konstantin Kosachev stating (and making no attempt whatsoever to hide the identity of the 'host' nation he was talking about), 'those who place missiles automatically and willingly, become a nuclear target with (just) several minutes of flight time'. So, let's be honest, this small island is seen as nothing more than a convenient warehouse by its so-called ally. A wet and draughty warehouse at that but one that is well out of the harm's way; if you're a US President, of course. None of them would, of course, ever have actively sought a Third World War but, had the balloon ever gone up, they would at least have got some comfort from the fact it would have taken place in and around Western Europe, rather than 'the land of the free and the home of the brave'. 'Special' relationship indeed.

The one-time NATO defence munitions department is a sizeable and complex facility that took four years to build and which, from 1989 onwards, served the alliance as a wartime ammunition depot with, it is quoted, around 40,000 tons worth of assorted weaponry including missiles, depth charges and conventional shells tucked away on the premises. Just take a moment or two now to think about that figure. And then, if you will, proceed briefly to the entry in this book about the SS *Richard Montgomery*, the partially submerged shipwreck (see 29) that lays on sandbank off the Essex coast. I write, in that section, of the possible damage that might be caused if the estimated 3,500 tons of explosive ordinance that remains on that ship was ever to go off, the bit that says, 'according to a study that was done by explosive experts, the biggest ever non-nuclear explosion in the history of mankind'. That's for 'just' 3,500 tons of explosive. Now multiply that number by around 11.5 and visualise the magnitude of the bang if DM Glen Douglas had ever blown up? All very simplistic of course. But the fact remains that having that amount of explosive material in one place is not good for anyone. Least of all, in this case, for much of Bute. They'd have seen and felt the explosion and shock wave in

Glasgow if Glen Douglas had gone off, even if Glasgow is nearly 40 miles away. Indeed, it's probably fair to say that, if it had ever happened, parts of Bute might well have ended up tumbling back down to earth over Glasgow.

MD Glen Douglas can't be missed to either the casual observer or an enemy spy satellite. It covers an area of nearly 700 acres with around sixty storage facilities contained within, each of which are built into the side of a hill. It is now used exclusively by the British military (which, given repeated cuts to the MoD from government, means there is probably nothing more than a couple of filing cabinets and some dried up bottles of Tipex stored behind it's formidable doors) and has, in more recent years, dispatched stored munitions to a jetty along the edge of nearby Loch Long, which is frequently visited by both Royal Navy and Royal Fleet Auxiliary vessels.

Operationally quieter than it was then. Which means the time to be worried would be if the amount of both traffic and personnel seen in and around the nearby B833 was ever to become a lot higher because places like this never close. They are forever in cold storage ready, if required, to assume their previous roles at very short notice indeed.

Distance view of the facility at Glen Douglas.

18. Gruinard Island, Inner Hebrides

Biological Warfare Testing Site

Now here's a thing. If you or I were to be seen dropping an empty packet of crisps or a sweet wrapper onto any street or the open countryside, there is every chance that someone armed with a clipboard and officious attitude might be able to issue us with a fine of up to £2,500. And, lest you all now think I'm a serial litterer, that's a sanction I heartily concur with. We live in a terribly untidy and litter strewn nation, so it is only right and fair that those who treat the great outdoors in the same casual manner they might regard their own homes are suitably brought to heel. But look. We all know that governments, all over the world, live by the mantra, 'do as I say, not as I do', which means that while DEFRA can spend time and money educating us all about why we mustn't despoil our surroundings, their masters at the very highest level of government can, at the same time, sanction the dropping of anthrax bombs onto a remote and beautiful Scottish island.

The motivation to do so came from the perceived threat that at some point in the Second World War if things weren't going terribly well for Nazi forces then they might, as an act of desperation, launch either chemical or biological attacks against either allied troops or civilians (i.e. British towns and cities). It was therefore not unreasonable, mused powers that be to, a) try to establish how effective and widespread an attack of that nature might be and, b) in the event of it ever taking place, having an effective response available in kind. This led to, in 1942, British scientists from Porton Down (see 33) heading off to the remote Gruinard Island which, after being successfully 'requisitioned' from its then owners (I find it hard to believe they were even remotely happy about having to do so), started carrying out tests of that nature on the island which culminated, over the summers of 1942 and 1943, with a Wellington aircraft dropping the anthrax-laden bombs on or nearby to some sheep that had been placed in open pens across the island. Inadvertently dropping your sweet wrapper onto the local high street doesn't seem quite such a big deal now, does it? The effect of the anthrax on the sheep was swift and deadly. They were all dead or dying within three days of the bombs having been dropped, with both the effectiveness of the weapon and the area that it ultimately covered leading to one report that followed these tests stating, with fiendish glee:

> The report of the Gruinard experiment indicated that biological weapons are highly effective and can paralyse or render cities inhospitable.

Can we assume from that brief and simple sentence that, if needed, a British Government would have sanctioned the dropping of biological weapons onto the civilian population of a city that, war or not, would have been the home of several hundred thousand non combatants? Presumably, had the need been somehow justified, they would have done just that? Fortunately, as the Second World War was, at this time, looking as if it would ultimately result in victory for the combined allied forces, the tests at Gruinard were ultimately abandoned. The owner duly requested that they be able to repurchase the island from the Government which, for £500, they were able to do with the caveat that they could not take back possession of the island until it was free of the contaminating anthrax spores. The British Government made, however, little to no attempt to clean up the deadly mess they'd made and for two decades after the end of the war tests on animals still living on the islands still showed traces of anthrax in their bodies.

Finally, in 1990, the British Government stage-managed a visit by a junior defence minister (why didn't they send Tom King, the then Minister of Defence?) who stood, smiling at the cameras, by the water's edge on the island as the signs that warned of its contamination were finally removed. It turned out to be a largely cosmetic exercise however, and nobody was fooled; the proof positive coming with the fact that, even today – three decades later – the Gruinard Island remains abandoned and barren, with the only visitors that it ever has being accidental ones.

Looking towards Gruinard Island from the 'safety' of the open water.

19. Hampstead Heath, London

River Fleet

The very mention of the word 'subterranean' can cause a little shudder of excitement to course through the body.

It implies darkness, mystery, the unknown and the very real chance of getting lost. Forever. H. G. Wells knew what he was doing when he wrote about the Morlocks in *The Time Machine*. They were very much the 'baddies' of the story, portrayed as the proverbial bug-eyed monsters who only emerged at night to either capture or feast upon the gentle surface-dwelling Eloi.

Stands to reason, thought Herbert. They live underground. So they must be bad.

It's doubtful that any monsters, Morlocks or otherwise, frequent the numerous tunnels and catacombs that thread their way throughout subterranean London. After all, many people are completely familiar with life underneath the capital, courtesy of the London Underground; the world's first underground passenger railway. But what about London's underground river?

Never heard of it? You won't be the only one. London has twenty-one subterranean rivers in all* with its largest, the River Fleet, rising as two separate streams on Hampstead Heath (both of which include the outdoor ponds on the heath that are so beloved of outdoor swimmers) before heading underground, flowing under Kentish Town before converging under Camden Town and flowing onwards toward St Pancras Old Church, which was once situated on the banks of the river. Not anymore. From there it adopts a sinuous route which, interestingly, is responsible for the otherwise unusual lines adopted by the buildings that sit adjacent to King's Cross mainline station with, in addition to that, the gentle curve of the Great Northern Hotel, which matches the course of the river that flows beneath it.

Incidentally, back in the glorious days when we had a national press to feel good about, what description was used as a collective reference for all of the great London dailies? That's right, Fleet Street. So now you know how Fleet Street got its name. That's because the eastern end of the street featured a crossing over the river known as Fleet Bridge, but which is now the site of Ludgate Circus.

The River Fleet then heads off down (but under) the King's Cross road and onto Clerkenwell before flowing down Farringdon Road and Farringdon Street where it broadens out before joining the River Thames beneath Blackfriars Bridge.

You can, if you wish, catch a quick glimpse of the River Fleet in London today if you go to Blackfriars Bridge and look for its drainage outlet on the Embankment wall. Alternately, you can listen to it flowing beneath your feet if you head for Ray Street in Clerkenwell and look down the iron grating that is situated in front of The Coach pub. If you are in London

---

* Four of them – the River Brent, River Rom, River Quaggy and Beverley Brook – are only partially subterranean.

on a particularly wet day, you also have the option of travelling to Blackfriars Station where, if the tidal state of the River Thames is low, you'll get to see the Fleet cascading into the Thames from the Thameswalk exit of Blackfriars Station, immediately under the bridge of the same name. Revel in it if you do. You're witnessing part of London's ancient history that, despite it being banished beneath the city's streets, lives on; an evocative reminder of the hidden worlds that lie, dark, dank and largely unexplored beneath our feet.

Left: Hampstead Heath from whence the River Fleet flows.

Below: Blackfriars bridge. Look out for the River Fleet entering the Thames here at low tide.

20. Harrogate, Yorkshire

RAF Menwith Hill

RAF Menwith Hill isn't just any old RAF station. You know, aircraft come in, aircraft head out, lots of noise and people with cameras and binoculars straining for a view from the perimeter fence.

Because it's a bit more than that. Indeed, it has been described as 'the largest electronic monitoring station in the world'.

Phew. And it's near Harrowgate, well known for Betty's Tea Rooms and its spring water; an elixir which pale and flighty types were first imbibing back in the sixteenth century. All very genteel and, well, English. But a hush-hush satellite ground station and incoming missiles warning site?

The base itself is owned by the MoD but has been freely available for use by the US Department of Defense since NATO drew up their Status of Forces Agreement (an agreement from a host nation to allow forces from another country to occupy share military facilities) in 1951. The US certainly have first dibs, so to speak, on what happens at RAF Menwith Hill as, although the aforementioned agreement (plus many others of a similar nature that exist between the two nations) grants possession of the site to Great Britain, its administration is the responsibility of the US authorities who manage its day to day running, coupled with the assistance of staff provided to them by GCHQ (see 8).

It's one of those 'arrangements' that you can tell isn't going to end well.

The base currently acts as a ground station for an unspecified number of satellites that are operated by the US National Reconnaissance Office ('spooks' in suits) on behalf of their National Security Agency, with their multi-million-dollar spying technology contained within a number of golf ball shaped buildings known as radomes. The whole set up is rumoured to be part of a worldwide surveillance programme that is operated and ran by the United States along with Australia, Canada, New Zealand and the United Kingdom. This global network is referred to as ECHELON (have you began to notice by now how much in love with acronyms the military are?), which was created in the late 1960s to run constant surveillance over all radio and similar communications made by the then Soviet Union and all of her Warsaw Pact allies. Which means you can probably bet your house that somewhere in Eastern Europe and probably in or around Siberia, there is an equivalent ran by Putin's Russia and his allies, including China, which constantly listens in to all the radio signals made by the United States and all of her NATO allies. As you can imagine, Yorkshire CND are not at all happy with what is going on at RAF Menwith Hill which is proving to be an increasingly large and sharp thorn in their sides. Perhaps their concerns should be shared by all of us?

They point to the widespread efforts made by US authorities to paint as positive a picture as possible with regard to the base and surrounding community – a difficult task, really, when you consider the aforementioned community will be on page one of any aggressive nations list of targets for a nuclear strike. Despite that, however, they stress just how much the base is worth in terms of the money its staff and contractors inject into Harrogate and the local area, with one quote suggesting the amount spent is in excess of over £100 million a year, which seems highly unlikely. They further point out that what is, at least publicly, an RAF base is really a very high-tech segment of the US military that has found itself a permanent home in the middle of the Yorkshire countryside one that, quote, 'carries out illegal forms of electronic spying and warfare over which there is no democratic accountability and very little debate'.

A point that I find is very difficult to disagree with.

A pastoral scene near Harrogate somewhat spoilt by the presence of the USA's radomes.

21. Huntingdon, Cambridgeshire

Huntingdon Life Sciences

If you were to ask anyone who worked at Huntingdon Life Sciences (HLS) exactly what they did, it's likely that their answer would include a reference to the fact that HLS are a 'contract research organisation' (CRO), which sounds a bit bland. So bland in fact that you are likely to move on at that point and engage them in some alternative form of debate; the weather, for example, or what's been happening on TV's *Sexy Island* or whatever the hell it's called. Which would suit the lady or gentleman in question very nicely. Yes, let's all move on and talk about something else. There's nothing to see here.

Except that, of course, there most definitely is because a CRO is defined as a company that provides support to each of the biological, medical device and pharmaceutical industries. That means they cover a host of services provided for some, which includes various commercial aspects relating to the product, but also those whose very mention tends to make some people rather worried, including clinical research and trials and also something referred to as pharmacovigilance.

Pharmacovigilance. It's quite a mouthful, but if you look to break the word down into its constituent parts, you can soon see what it refers to. Pharma = medicine or drugs, and vigilance = safety and care. So, it's all about making sure that the medicine we take is not only effective in treating the underlying condition, but that it's also safe to take. So, for example, say your doctor prescribes you something you've never taken before. Most people will, upon opening the packet, take out the piece of paper that's been put in there along with the medicine that contains everything you ever needed to know about it which, inevitably, includes a list of possible side effects that may be experienced after taking it common, rare or otherwise.

Pharmacovigilance in action.

Except of course there are numerous ways and means of finding out if a medical product is safe to take. This ranges from asking people to sign up for clinical trials (not something I'd be in favour of doing, having just the one head suits me fine) or, as is frequently alleged, testing them on animals. Hence the reason that HLS is a rather secretive and very secure place because, as far as most well adjusted people are concerned, that is simply not on.

If you want to take the risk of signing up to be a human guinea pig, then so be it. We all have free will and said risks are made very clear to us beforehand. And they must be there because people who did partake in such trials are often, upon their completion, paid very generous amounts of money for their time and trouble. It's one of the great examples of real 'danger money' being paid. But testing products on a real guinea pig or any other innocent animal, be it cat, dog, rabbit, hamster or any other species other than ourselves, just seems to be very wrong, and understandably so.

by-sa/2.0 - What's round the corner? by Christine Johnstone - geograph.org.uk/p/213

Huntingdon Life Sciences and a perimeter fence that doesn't invite suspicion at all!

According to one campaigning website*, HLS have housed up to 70,000 animals on site. Just sit down and think about that for a minute. That's roughly the population of Lowestoft. Is that right? Is our own health and well being so important that we feel we can use animals in this way, to virtually enslave them in order to serve our complicated and self-absorbed twenty-first century lives?

That's an argument for another day and another book. But the controversy that has always raged about testing on animals, and the antagonism that even the idea that it might be happening stirs up in people, goes a long – long – way to explain why HLS is one of the most security conscious and, for those very reasons, secretive non-military organisations in the United Kingdom today.

---

* www.change.org

22. Hyde Park Corner, London

Lanesborough Hotel

First things first. This isn't a hotel. Well yes, it is, but it doesn't like to have the word 'hotel' included in any or narrative written about it. For, much as the All England Lawn Tennis Championships is simply referred to as 'Wimbledon' and the British Open Golf Championship is known as 'The Open', the super rich and powerful who own and run the Lanesborough Hotel would prefer it if one simply referred to it as 'The Lanesborough'.

I'm never going to get a free night's stay by indulging them here but anyway, The Lanesborough it is.

It sits, rather like a becalmed ocean liner, on Hyde Park Corner, a symbol of wealth, privilege and greed. Untouchable to the likes of you and I who, at least, have a little bit of taste about our person but, for all that, a shining beacon of olde world class distinction for its patrons, many of whom, I am sure, would still force young children to climb up chimneys or crawl under a spinning jenny, given half the chance. Ironic then that the building started life as a hospital where, unlike its present incarnation, anyone would be more than welcome. I wonder then if, in honour of its medical past, The Lanesborough has rooms that have been given names in honour of its former, most noble role? The Forceps Suite maybe, or possibly the Tuberculosis Dining Room?

The hospital is now in Tooting, having been relocated there in 1980 while the old building, now in the hands of the Abu Dhabi Investment Authority, was converted into London's most prestigious hotel at an estimated cost of around £80 million, which buys a lot of lavish. More than you'd ever need but then, in for a penny, in for a million pounds, as its owners might like to say. It must be an absolute nightmare to maintain and keep in the splendour to which it is now accustomed. This is a hotel which, after all, doesn't get the builders in to slap a bit of emulsion on tired corridor walls, or just lay one of those incredibly bright and garish carpets that most standard hotels seem to favour (and why is that?), but one that opts for individual hand paintings stencilled onto wood in each and every one of the bathrooms. Put it another way, there are no prints of pre-Raphaelite paintings on the walls here, not unless it's the original.

You've probably heard that some of the grander hotels offer a butler service for some of its more upmarket rooms? The Savoy, for example, does so for each of its suites. The Lanesborough, on the other hand, offers a butler for every room. So no matter where you might be tucked away in its spectacular interior, you'll always have access to your very own Jeeves. But that's not all. The Lanesborough is home to its very own Michelin-starred restaurant, and offer an award-winning afternoon tea service and an in-house club and spa facility.

Plus, to top it all off, one of (so they claim to say) 'London's best cigar and Cognac lounges'. Well, that's ruined it for me I'm afraid, if the whole place reeks of stale cigar smoke, then I'm just not interested.

Top of the pile at The Lanesborough is The Royal Suite, seven bedrooms in total including, of course, tea and coffee making facilities. Though I'm guessing the coffee may not be instant or, for that matter, that you would be expected to make it yourself. Fittingly, it offers views of Buckingham Palace gardens from its ornate windows; rooms with a view that, as well as the seven bedrooms already mentioned, also include two living rooms and a dining room for up to twelve guests. You'll also (lucky things) have access to your very own chauffeur-driven car as part of your booking. So, no changing at Green Park for Hyde Park Corner tube then.

How much? The Lanesborough, not surprisingly, consider it somewhat vulgar to display a price for such luxury. So, to use the old adage, if you have to ask how much it is, then you can't afford it. You can, however, assume that it'll be a five-figure sum.

The somewhat 'OTT' Lanesborough Hotel in London.

23. Kelvedon Hatch, Essex

Secret Nuclear Bunker

The location of this nuclear bunker used to be about as secure and secret as anywhere in the entire country. Understandable really, as its ultimate purpose would have been to have served as a regional government hub in the event of a nuclear attack else some other dire national emergency (e.g. cataclysmic weather conditions or the nation's supermarkets running out of sprouts in the run up to Christmas).

On a more serious note, the reasons that facilities such as these went to great time and expense to keep their locations secret wasn't so much about hoping to escape being targeted by an enemy missile or two (rest assured, there would have been a mole somewhere in Whitehall who would have revealed their locations to their Soviet paymasters), but to try and prevent mass ingress by thousands upon thousands of members of the general public, who had worked out it was their one chance of surviving the coming conflagration.

Because you don't want to be wasting your time fending them all off, by deadly force if possible, when the purpose of a facility such as this, was to try and establish some sort of post-war order.

Kelvedon Hatch (KH) was built in 1952 as part of an intensive programme to improve Britain's air defence network and was designated, in the first instance, as an operations centre for the London sector, assuming there was anything left of London, of fighter command. It remained in use as regional defence site until the early 1990s when, with the threat of nuclear war widely believed to have receded (that sounds a bit premature now), the bunker and the land it stood upon was sold back to the original owner.

And its most definitely not a 'top secret' location anymore. Infact you can now go and visit it.

One of the most delightful things about the site is its postal address because the first line of it includes the words 'Secret Nuclear Bunker', which is wonderful.

You can also hire the space for a corporate 'do', or, failing that, if you are a film maker looking for somewhere dark and sinister from where you can shoot the end of the world, then Kelvedon Nuclear Bunker has everything you'll ever need for the claustrophobic feel that you will want your movie to project.

The tour of the bunker is self guided and taken with the help of personal headsets. The tour includes several films to watch as you wend your way into the ground as well as a dressing up area where the curious visitor can try on an assortment of military uniforms, as well as a gas mask or two. Not surprisingly, given that it is, practically speaking, a big hole in the ground, the site owner has pointed out that there is limited access for disabled people.

Which is a bit of a shame for present day wheelchair users. But, chillingly, it says a lot about the approach to disabled people at the time in the event of a conflict and the need to find shelter as soon as possible, as no provision seems to have been made for them. What were they meant to do, just accept their fate?

Ultimately, Kelvedon was designed for up to 600 military and civilian personnel to take shelter, including, given its proximity to London, the Prime Minister and all of the members of his/her cabinet. Their task would have been a grim one, an expectation to deliver the impossible and try to organise the survival of those members of the population that had survived a nuclear attack on this country.

A time when Kelvedon Hatch (population approx. 2,500) might, temporarily, have been the nation's capital.

Above: The unassuming entrance to the top-secret nuclear bunker at Kelvedon Hatch.

Left: Access tunnel at Kelvedon Hatch.

Above left: One of the extremely strong blast proof doors at Kelvedon Hatch.

Above right: A generator at Kelvedon Hatch.

Rear staircase at Kelvedon Hatch –
a way out that might never have
been needed?

24. Longniddry, East Lothian

Seton Castle

Looking to move house? Need a bit more space, perhaps? That or thinking you might get a little more bricks and mortar for your money if you sell your five-bedroom detached place in leafy Surrey and move 'up north'?

Then your quest is over. Or, rather, it might have been if you were doing the endless rounds with the estate agents (and aren't they cumberworlds; one once tried to convince me a coal shed would make a 'wonderfully bijou downstairs WC') in the summer of 2019.

Because that is when Seton Castle was on the market, which at the time of writing remains the case. So what better chance to own one of the most exclusive properties in the UK, one that, among other things, was a popular retreat for Mary, Queen of Scots and which was built in the latter years of the eighteenth century, after the previous building on the site, Seton Palace, was demolished. The latter had a grand reputation as being one of the most magnificent – inside and out – buildings in Scotland; a site and sight that, sadly, burnt down during the Jacobite Rising in 1715.

How do you replace such splendour?

It took three years to do so but it is fair to say that the castle that rose from the ashes of the palace more than did justice to its predecessor and would, as it does now, have encouraged many a prying eye or enquiring footstep or two within its newly built but exclusive walls. Unfortunately Seton Castle, because it remains a private dwelling, is not a location that the general public can explore and, in the process, lose themselves in the majesty and mystique of its fairytale façade and glorious grounds. Which is a great pity as, in my opinion, the very best chance for great buildings to survive and prosper is for them to be freely available for all to see and, in the process, immerse themselves in local events that, in many cases, ended up having a long lasting effect on a far wider area.

Seton Castle deserves to be more than a billionaire's occasional weekend indulgence, its perimeter scarred with 'Keep Out' signs and CCTV cameras. It's rich with period Georgian features, boasts décor that goes beyond opulent, fabrics and all manner of hues in abundance, a building at ease with itself and how very special it is. You can, of course, attempt to buy class (see 22) but when it comes naturally and as if little to no effort has been made to display it, then all you can do is step back and give the architect a round of applause for creating something so very wonderful.

In Seton's case, the gentleman in question was one Robert Adam. His CV makes for impressive reading as his mark is also recorded upon the world famous Pulteney Bridge in Bath; Old College at the University of Edinburgh, Fitzroy Square in London and, also in London, Osterley Park – one of the biggest open spaces in the capital and famous for being the first training grounds of the Home Guard during the Second World War.

If there isn't a statue of this man somewhere then there should be.

Seton remains one of Adam's masterpieces, architectural majesty and a visual treat that should be available for all to see and drink in, rather than a privileged few. I rather suspect its asking price of around £8,000,000 is a little too steep for The National Trust of Scotland to be able to afford but regardless of what happens to Seton over the coming years and decades, the very lamentable fact that it is a prize available only to the very few and is therefore as forbidden a place as any in this book is a regrettable one.

The rather lovely Seaton Castle.

25. Lothians, Scottish Lowlands

Secret Tunnel under River Forth

If I was asked to describe the Forth Bridge in just one word, I'd have a problem with which one I'd ultimately choose. Spectacular? Iconic? Eye-catching? Beautiful? The list goes on and on. It is one of the most recognisable bridges in the world with, for me, its greatest appeal being that it is not only a great feat of engineering, it looks like one as well. It wasn't a rushed job either. The bridge took eight years to build, is 8,094 feet long and, for a time, it had the longest single cantilever bridge span in the world.

It's also, of course, the focus of a familiar and well worn saying, one that is inevitably dragged out whenever someone mentions a never ending task of one kind or another, adding that 'it's like painting the Forth Bridge', i.e. an endless job with, as legend has it, the job taking so long that once its entire length has been covered by a nice new coat of glass flake epoxy (you don't slap everyday emulsion on this sort of structure) paint, the decorators have then got to go back to the beginning and start all over again. There was an element of truth in that phrase up until 2011 when Network Rail, who own the bridge, claimed the world's longest ever paint job was finally finished and that the bridge wouldn't need painting again for twenty-five years. It's a structure made for superlatives. But figure this out. If the concept, construction and day to day management of the bridge is one thing, then how about that of the matching tunnel which runs under, rather than over the River Forth?

The subterranean Forth crossing was opened in 1964 at a depth of over 1500 feet below sea level when, after what must have been one of the toughest, arduous and potentially dangerous engineering achievements ever made in modern Scotland, coal miners from the Kinneil Colliery, built on the south side of the river, met up with their peers from the Valleyfield Colliery in Fife. Their meeting up, in conditions that would have been pitch black, claustrophobic beyond belief (certainly to the likes of you and me) and uncomfortably humid meant that, for the first time in history and certainly before the world famous bridge way, above their heads was opened, it was now possible to walk directly from the Lothians to Fife without getting your feet wet or needing to take a boat. Astonishing stuff. So why do so few people know about it? Well for a start, it was never intended to be built and left for pedestrians to make their way under the river from one side to the other. It didn't need to be bright, airy, spacious and comfortable. It merely had to serve a purpose which was at the time purely an economic one in this case, allowing for the coal that was dug from the rich seams in Fife to be easily dispatched southwards for processing in Fife, rather than at the old fashioned and somewhat decrepit facility that was already in existence at Valleyfield. The tunnel also had the additional 'perk' of increasing the working lives of a further three coalfields as whatever was mined there could also be transported through the tunnel.

Sadly, no visible evidence of the tunnel remains. Both Kinneil and Valleyfield Colliery's have long been demolished as has, of course, the entire industry of which they both played an important and noble part. As for actual documentary evidence of the tunnel, it now only exists on a few maps and plans as well as a few photographs. So, anyone seeking the thrill of descending into the bowels of the earth here for an underground challenge like no other will be disappointed, primarily because the mine shafts leading to the tunnel have been backfilled for eternity with hardcore before being capped in concrete. Even the iron props used to maintain the tunnels structure will have buckled under the tremendous load they have had to bear, while in other parts of the tunnel floor to roof levels will have been flooded with groundwater. The site is, to all extents and purposes, lost forever.

It was planned at a time when the world had no shortage of visionaries and excavated by men who were as strong and unyielding as the rock they had to hack and hew their way through. A once forbidding place where you could have walked to Fife and back underneath the sea, a fact as startling to believe as the Forth Bridge is to behold.

The Forth Bridge, a remarkable engineering achievement. But not as impressive as the fact a tunnel was built under the river near here.

26. Lulworth, Dorset

MoD Military Ranges

A beautiful part of the country.

Sweeping views across a verdant landscape and cliffs that soar ever upwards from a deep blue sea. If you're old enough to remember *This England* magazine, it's a view that would have graced any cover.

Maybe that's why the MoD like Dorset so much? It means they can play at their war games while admiring the scenery in the process. I'm sure there are plenty of places in England that, in the minds of certain people, are far more deserving of being a testing ground for missiles but look, few will be as relaxing as Lulworth.

Chill as you kill.

The ranges at Lulworth are used by the Armoured Fighting Vehicles Gunnery School who are a training establishment within the British Army. The area used, which spreads east of the glorious Lulworth Cove to west of Kimmeridge Bay is heavily restricted during firing times. When the range is in use, red warning flags are shown as well as brightly lit lamps, both of which act as highly visible deterrents to any curious walkers who might otherwise have strayed into the danger zone. But it doesn't begin and end at that (besides, when you think about it, red flags and warning lamps seem more suitable to the dawn of the railways, when they might have been used to warn the public that a mighty engine was about to roar past them at all of 10 mph) as the MoD also provides information that can be accessed by ringing a recorded information service that will provide up to date news on what is happening on the range, as well as when the area it contains (which includes two villages and the remains of a 185 million year old fossil forest) is open to the general public.

The ranges were first established in 1917 and cover an area of around 7,000 acres. One of the aforementioned villages that stands within the range area is Tyneham, which is now a ghost village, having been handed over to the military in 1943 before the Army completed a compulsory purchase of the village in 1948. It is, at least, now a thriving nature reserve but does, to this day, remain in use as a practice battleground for the military and is listed as having an official population of zero.

The story of Tyneham is a very sad one, a testament of course to the power that lies in the hands of a government that can forcibly remove people from their homes. Unfortunately for the village, the development of ever more powerful weapons in the decades that followed the First World War meant that it was now, in the eyes of the MoD, 'in the way'. The Government were hardly going to pack their things away and find somewhere else to test the latest tanks and related hardware, so Tyneham became expendable and is now a traditional English village that is, for the most part, forbidden to unofficial visitors.

When the last of the villagers left Tyneham, one of them left a handwritten note on the door of St Mary's Church, which read:

Please treat the church and houses with care; we have given up our homes where many of us lived for generations to help with the war (and) to keep men free. We shall return one day and thankyou for treating the village kindly.

Tragically, the people of Tyneham never did get to return to their village and, although the church is still standing and has been recently restored, much of the rest of Tyneham lays in ruins.

A sure sign that the technology being tested is up to the job, but at a considerable human cost.

A subtle warning as to the potential dangers of walking near Lulworth.

27. Lympstone Commando Railway Station, Devon

Railway Station for 'Exclusive' use of Royal Marines

You may, as I most certainly am, be a bit of a devotee of rail travel and all things train related. If you also like to explore, armed with only a map, bottle of water and stout pair of boots and like to marry the former with the latter, then the network of railways that await you in England's glorious west country are a rich haven indeed.

But this is one station you won't be alighting at with thoughts of a peaceful days pootling about the place. Although if you did or, more relevantly, had reason to be there, then the stout boots would, at least, come in handy. That's because Lympstone Commando Railway Station, situated on the branch line from Exeter to Exmouth, is, or rather was, private and for the exclusive use of visitors to the nearby Royal Marine Commando Training Centre. So, there is no little kiosk on the platform, no waiting room or friendly member of staff available to check your tickets. Just a stark platform and a wire fence, crowned with barbed wire that most certainly isn't standard Network Rail issue. Plus, if it's your first day, a scary man whose sole purpose in life is to scream and shout at you 24/7 from now on but look, at least he met you off the train. Bless. Just don't expect him to carry your bags for you.

It is, to be fair, a rather attractive place. The single platform overlooks water while, on either side, the embankments are green and lush, full of flora and fauna with enough variety of bird song to please any ornithologist. In short, a destination you could stay at for a while, rest weary legs and slake your thirst from a dangling Thermos. You could even, if you close your eyes, forget that you were right on top of the training HQ of one of the most respected and elite fighting forces in the world. Harsh reality bites, however, if your eyes are drawn upwards to the forbidding red sign that is visible to all along the platform, the one that states, 'Persons Who Alight Here Must Only Have Business with the Camp'.

The only exit from the station was originally through a locked gate into the Commando base but this has, in recent years, been modernised by way of a footpath that enables easier access to and from the station from the base. It does remain, however, the only place you can go to from Lympstone Commando, so unless you have a very genuine reason to be there don't even think about wandering in for a look around, as the security team won't look upon you at all kindly for doing so.

Lympstone Commando station was opened in 1976. The attractive views that it affords are due to the fact it overlooks the River Exe, not that you'll have anytime to admire it once you arrive. It is a request stop only which means that, if you are due to get off at the station on a train travelling up from Exeter, you must advise a member of train crew of your wish at the start of your journey. Similarly, if you are at the station and wish, for whatever reasons, to catch a train from it, then it is advisable to make your intentions known to the driver as he or she approaches the platform.

The station is not, contrary to popular belief, the property of the Ministry of Defence but does in fact belong to Network Rail, a fact that have led to the MoD admitting that they have no power or right to stop curious members of the general public from alighting there. They do, however, point out that anyone acting in a suspicious manner on the platform (e.g. taking photographs) would immediately attract the rather keen and enthusiastic attentions of the stations security staff, who would, in all likelihood, invite you to accompany them to the wrong side of the adjacent security fence that surrounds the site.

Which might put a bit of a dampener on your day out.

If you alight here, you must be about to join the Royal Marines. Good luck!

28. Monte Bello Islands, Indian Ocean

British Nuclear Weapon Testing Site

Ernest Bevin has got a lot to answer for. He was a Labour politician and Trade Union leader who co-founded and served as the General Secretary of the Transport & General Workers Union (TGWU) from 1922 to 1940, as well as serving in the wartime coalition government as the Minister of Labour. You would think, therefore, that as a man of, shall we say political inclinations that leaned somewhat to the left of centre, he'd be anti-war and a man of peace? Well, no. Not really. Because he was the man, in October 1946, a little over a year after the US military had dropped their newly acquired atomic bombs onto the Japanese cities of Hiroshima and Nagasaki, who said that as far as that most terrible of weapons was concerned 'we've got to have the bloody thing over here, whatever it costs ... we've got to have the bloody Union Jack on top of it'. Not everyone agreed with him, especially Hugh Dalton, the then Chancellor, and Stafford Cripps, President of the Board of Trade, who would in time succeed Dalton at 11 Downing Street. Powerful political adversaries. Yet Bevin got his way and work on Britain's atomic bomb started, done in such a clandestine manner that not all of Bevin's colleagues on the cabinet were even aware of it. Rapid progress was made and, by the time that the Conservatives (under Churchill) were back in power, all that was left to be done was the test the new weapon.

One disadvantage that the British immediately had was exactly where they would test their new weapon. The US military did, at least, have vast tracts of empty space 'in house' where their bombs could be detonated with locations in Alaska and Nevada initially used. The British Government had no such option to call upon and had, as an alternative, to seek a suitable location elsewhere in the world where they might safely (relatively speaking) detonate the countries first nuclear bomb. This turned out to be on the uninhabited Monte Bello Islands off the north-west coast of Australia. The area in and around the islands were duly declared a prohibited zone with ships and aircraft operating in the region warned not to enter an area of just under 24,000 nautical square miles in and around the islands. Subtle, as you can see, it most certainly wasn't and the eyes of the world, including those of the UK's enemies, would most definitely been focused on this previously obscure part of world. Thus, with numerous servicemen in attendance on either adjoining islands or as part of the accompanying fleet of British and Australian Naval ships looking on (although they were told to face away from the initial blast due to the intensely bright light it would create at the point of detonation), the bomb exploded, instantly vaporising (in the process) HMS *Pym*, the frigate in which it had been kept. A few white-hot pieces of metal were flung skyward, eventually falling onto one of the islands and starting a number of fires. The explosion itself caused a rapidly spreading grey cloud to a height of 10,000 feet within 2 minutes, this cloud eventually extending 2 miles upwards, while it measured over a mile across at its base. For those watching from far away, the physical effects of the bomb could be felt after 4 minutes with a sound not unlike that of a thunderclap and shockwave that rattled windows.

This first test (of many in the region) had been, the British Government declared, a 'great success'. A sentiment that could not be shared by the British servicemen, totalling around 22,000, who witnessed this and subsequent tests in the area. They might have had their backs to the bombs as they went off, but this didn't stop them feeling the intense heat given off by the explosion as they had no protective clothing provided, with one veteran telling the BBC in 2018 that he felt he and his colleagues were nothing more than guinea pigs adding, 'it was so bright I could see the bones in my hands with my eyes closed. It was like an X-ray'. Many of them believe being so close to the test sites has ended up causing numerous health problems for both themselves and their families (e.g. cancers, fertility problems and birth defects) that are now being passed down through the generations.

I'm sure they will all have had some comfort in knowing that Bevin's 'bloody thing' at least had a Union Jack on it.

A memorial to those who died as a consequence of the British nuclear testing programme in the Indian Ocean.

29. Off Sheerness, Kent

SS *Richard Montgomery*

Images of shipwrecks are always evocative. Regardless of whether the ship in question might have been the most humble of sea faring craft or as world famous as *Titanic* (and who hasn't found their breath being snatched away at the first sight of its mighty bow looming up in her final resting place?), there is always an accompanying story and they're rarely, if ever, happy ones.

SS *Richard Montgomery* (SS *RM*) has laid, inert, on a sandbank off Sheerness for a little over seventy-five years now. Yet, rusting hulk that she is, the real story relating to her is not so much about what happened to her one night in 1944 but what might still happen to her.

SS *RM* was one of 2,710 'Liberty Ships' built in the USA in order to provide essential supplies to the war effort from across the Atlantic. They had a short lifespan – no more than five years – but during the time would be expected to carry thousands of tons of material to destinations all over Europe. She set sail from the US in the Summer of 1944, fully loaded with 7,000 tons of high explosives, a deadly cargo that included a number of 1,000 lb bombs. She had an uneventful Atlantic crossing (can you imagine how nervous you would be sailing on a ship that contains 7,000 tons of high explosives?) and arrived at Southend, her final destination, before a planned crossing of the English Channel for Cherbourg; this part of the journey now dependent on her waiting for a convoy to accompany her on the trip. She therefore needed an overnight mooring off the Essex coast and was directed by the Harbour Master to make for an area known as the Great North Anchorage to do so. This decision was duly challenged by the Deputy Harbour Master who, aware of the enormous weight of her cargo, felt that it was, given how shallow the waters were at that point, an unsuitable mooring location. He was, however, overruled and took his challenge no further.

His caution was understandable. SS *RM* was heading for a mooring that, at low tide, had a depth of less than 30 feet, while the fully loaded draft of SS *RM* was around 31 feet. Things were, clearly, not going to end well and the Deputy Harbour Master had already worked that out for himself. The ship anchored and overnight started to drift towards the shallow waters of the sandbanks. This was noted by the members of other craft in the vicinity who sounded warnings in her direction, but these were steadfastly ignored by the Officer of the Watch who didn't even bother to wake his sleeping Captain up in order to at least appraise him of the potential situation. SS *RM* ran aground in on the sandbank which meant that she would be left there for two weeks, the time it would take for a high enough tide to float her off again, providing that all of her cargo was removed. This work commenced but, over time, the stresses on the ships body led to her breaking in half and sinking atop the sandbank she had drifted onto.

With no-one knowing exactly what to do next, the wreck was eventually abandoned, and she remains there today. Part of her superstructure is still visible above the dark and cold waters of the Thames Estuary, complete, still, with 3,500 tons of high explosives sealed within her sunken hold, explosives that could quite feasibly and at any given time explode. If this was to happen it would be, according to a study that was done by explosive experts, the biggest ever non-nuclear explosion in the history of mankind, one that would send enormous chunks of molten steel and iron up to 2 miles in the air and create a tidal wave that would be at least 40 feet high; big enough to cause considerable damage along the coast and in London as it surged up river, overwhelming the Thames Flood Barrier (not that there would be time to put the barriers into place).

Damage and loss of life on an incalculable basis, or as one local resident has opined, 'biblical'. Yet in spite of all that the residents of Sheerness and the neighbouring towns all get on with their lives as normal. 'Monty', as she is referred to, is a part of their daily lives and one that is, for many, still visible. But what else can they do but, as one wartime phrase famously stated, 'keep calm and carry on'?

The masts of the SS *Richard Montgomery* peeking above the waters of the Thames Estuary.

30. Orford Ness, Suffolk

Atomic Weapons Research Establishment Test Buildings

If ever there was a location specifically designed for tens of thousands of A-Level Geography students to visit, year upon year, then it's this one.

Orford Ness off the Suffolk coast, the largest vegetated shingle spit in Europe, stretches for around 10 miles in length with a maximum height above sea level of just 13 feet. You can almost see the sodden notebooks and drooping sandwiches now. It's no Aldeburgh or Southwold, it's not even a Felixstowe, because Orford Ness has, for various reasons, always been a lonely and somewhat underrated spot, one that, up to the early 1900s, was solely used for animal grazing on the spits reclaimed marshland. A wild and desolate place, as Private Fraser from *Dad's Army* might have said.

That is until 1915 when, energised by the possibilities that seemed to be offered by aircraft in warfare (the B.E.2 biplane, for example, had primarily been used in reconnaissance roles), the Royal Flying Corps* constructed an airstrip on part of the reclaimed marshes, together with an assortment of buildings intended for logistical and other support services. They also laid a stretch of railway track which ran from the airfield to a jetty, ideal for bringing supplies in by boat and swiftly transporting them over to the airfield, which was dedicated to not only testing new aircraft as well but the armaments that came with them, including machine guns and bombs. The site was also used for a range of research related projects intended to improve the effectiveness of the aeroplane which was, at that time, a raw novice as far as its application in the theatre of war was concerned.

It didn't take long for the 'powers that be' to work out that, as Orford Ness was, even for East Anglia, a relatively remote and unpopulated spot, it could be usefully engaged as a site for the testing of ballistics (i.e. bombs) which could be dropped onto it without really bothering anyone and certainly not provoking letters from angry residents had they, for example, opted to do so in the aforementioned and nearby Aldeburgh. So, to paraphrase the words of the mighty John Betjeman, the invitation went out to 'come friendly bombs and fall on Orford Ness' with testing on ballistics of that nature continuing into the 1950s and beyond as the Atomic Weapons Research Establishment used the site for environmental testing, which simulated the conditions that a nuclear weapon might experience during actual service use. In other words, they needed to consider whether or not the performance of a nuclear weapon might have been affected if the poor thing, bless it, was too cold, hot, damp or just having a bad day in general. The legacy of the MoD's long presence at Orford Ness are the remains of several structures that still litter its otherwise featureless landscape to this day. One of those is known as the Control Room and Hard Target (latter pictured) which, as its name suggests, was designed and built as

---

* Later the Royal Air Force.

Above: One of the 'impact facilities' at Orford Ness.

Right: Inside one of the many mysterious structures at Orford Ness.

what is euphemistically referred to as an 'impact facility'. I'll leave you, wise reader, to work out what that might mean. The fact that, as the photograph shows, this particular structure looks relatively undamaged suggests that the bombs that were either dropped onto, or launched at it, were not exactly the most powerful available at the time.

Can you visit Orford Ness today? Indeed you can, although access is limited in terms of when the spit (which is currently owned and administered by the National Trust) is open to visitors and how you can reach it, given that access is usually by way of a ferry, which is also provided by the National Trust. So, check their website for more details. Rest assured, however, that the whole area retains an air of mystery and can be, at the best of times, a very atmospheric place to explore. It is also, for once, given the National Trust's interest in this particular landscape, one that has had nothing whatsoever to do with Capability Brown, which makes a change.

31. Ottershaw, Surrey

Queenswood Golf Club

Few social pursuits twist and torment the blood quite like the noble game of golf.

If you're not a fan then much more often than not you resent the very idea that thousands of acres of prime countryside should be set aside in order for privileged few to indulge in an expensive and inaccessible game, and that's your choice. But it isn't a sport for the 'privileged few' – not anymore anyway. This is because England boasts the most golf courses of any country in Europe, a total of 1,872 that are shared among at least 2 million active players, many of which will be members of a club.

Yet it is a game that can rile the devotee just as much. Broken clubs, golf bags hurled into lakes, running arguments and fall outs, they all happen on a golf course. It's a game renowned for its belief in 'proper' etiquette at all times, but, for all that, in the bunker, no-one can hear you scream.

I should add at this point I do have a vested interest. I play the game myself and have, in the past, been a member of a club. And I'm neither wealthy nor privileged. Indeed, it is a game that, despite its elitist image, is open to all to explore and play should they wish.

Sounds positively utopian, doesn't it? Sadly, however, there are still bastions of inaccessibility within the game, clubs and facilities that are so jealously guarded by their members that, in some cases, you might find the penalties for trespassing onto any part of their hallowed acres even more severe than if you were caught inside RAF Menwith Hill (see 20) with a camera, notepad and several known acquaintances of Kim-Jong-un.

One such establishment is the Queenswood Golf Club near Ottershaw in Surrey.

It is, in many ways, very untypical of a British golf club. Its whole approach to both members and their guests, from the moment they pass through its secure gates, is one of slick professionalism and sheer panache. Nothing is too much trouble. It's not unlike arriving at one of the best hotels in the world. Your baggage (or in this case golf clubs) are taken from you upon arrival (valet parking, of course) and sent to the first tee where they will await your arrival. If your golf shoes need cleaning, then they'll attend to that for you as well while you can forget hauling your own clubs across the green swathe as a caddy will always be provided. It's high end all the way; a millionaire's playground for the wealthy with no expense spared. Does such a philosophy, dare I say it, go against the spirit of the game? Well yes, absolutely, it definitely does. But when even the clubs website requires a login and password to access it (in comparison, GCHQ, for goodness sake, is on Twitter!) you know you are entering a place where there is no such thing as normality, average or, gasp, off the shelf.

This is golf in the most grandeur of settings, and if you want it you are going to have to pay for it. The joining fee alone is rumoured to be six figures with an article about the club that featured in GQ magazine (now there's a publication that would never be allowed to taint the clubhouse) back in 2017, claiming that it was around £200,000. So, goodness only knows what it is now. That hasn't prevented, indeed, the excess which is probably what encouraged numerous celebrities (whose names I have but I'll be beggared if I am going to give them a mention here) to join the club, one for whom a spokesman said in the aforementioned article, 'We don't like to talk about our club or who our members are or how much it costs'. Well, not to the 'hoi polloi' anyway. But you can bet your last bottle of Juglar Cuvee it's all they talk about out on the course.

It's golf Sebastian. But not as we know it.

Queenswood Golf Club is so security conscious, we had to take to the air for a photograph!

32. Pickering, Yorkshire

RAF Fylingdales Ballistic Missile Early Warning System (BMEWS)

Think of a *Star Wars* film, part XXI perhaps*. Our intrepid heroes are trudging across a wet and unforgiving landscape, all grey skies and scudding clouds, mists and moor. They are feeling as if there is no hope left when, suddenly, out of the murk emerges a building, its dirty white appearance in keeping with the surrounding dank. Their spirits, previously low, now hit rock bottom as 80-Ring, the droid that has been accompanying them announces in a dull voice, 'Oh dear. We seem to have found the HQ of the Dark Lords of the Sith' because RAF Fylingdales does look sinister. Infact it's probably the scariest looking of all the locations in this book. The sort of place that demands a second and even a third glance. You might end up thinking you'd rather be anywhere but on the periphery of this strange alien looking landscape, but then it compels you to look once again and to wonder just what on earth is going on inside those tenebrific structures? The MoD is, as always, completely open about RAF Fylingdales and its role, or at least the role it feels comfortable with us knowing about, which has never been that much of a secret. It provides a 24/7 early warning system to both the UK and US governments (it's only by researching and writing a book of this nature that you begin to realise how very closely intertwined the two are) in the event of a ballistic missile attack on either country. The overall objective of the site means being able to detect one in enough time for some sort of response to be offered including, naturally, a retaliatory one. Thus, the last act of RAF Fylingdales and, indeed, Yorkshire in general, would be to confirm incoming missiles before the whole site becomes a very large, very deep and exceedingly hot crater.

Let's hope someone on their first day doesn't detect a murmuration of starlings and think it's an incoming ICBM.

There can be, of course, no down time for any of the 350 or so staff that work at the site. 24/7 means that their dedication to their role has to be total, no matter what might be happening on the outside world, which is just as well when you consider that (among many other examples) an inadequate response to the looming danger of the Japanese forces was one of the reasons why the attack on Pearl Harbour in 1941 is regarded as a 'surprise' one. 'Be Prepared' may well be the motto of the Scout movement, but it equally applies to Fylingdales and its objective of ensuring that the UK, USA and their allies are never caught 'on the hop' by enemy forces again because the hardware they have to call upon is mightily impressive. The site's Ballistic Missile Early Warning Stations (BMEWS) can track objects in space that are up to 3,000 nautical miles away, while the station's radar operators are able to see the International Space Station, as well as objects that are the size of a can of Coca Cola. This means that, as much as they'd like an attack to be subtle and go undetected, there is little to no chance of a three stage ICBM that weighs

---

* *Star Wars* pt. XXI – 'When Will This Ever End?'

Left: Now you know what a phased array radar structure looks like. RAF Fylingdales.

Below: As close as you can get to the fence at RAF Fylingdales.

several tons and is travelling at speeds in excess of 10,000 mph sneaking in through the back door. So, we should all be grateful that we'll at least get a warning of our impending doom. But then that warning isn't, of course, for the likes of you and me. We are, in the event of this dread event happening, little more than collateral. The warning is for our own forces to have that time to decide how they want to respond.

Perhaps the most famous landmarks at RAF Fylingdales were the three 'golf ball' radar buildings. These have long been superseded by the new phased array radar structure that has the appearance of a three sided pyramid, which has been operational since 1992 and which is a very familiar landmark to those who travel on the adjacent road to and from Whitby, which was, incidentally, the original home of Bram Stoker's Count Dracula.

Even his castle couldn't have been as foreboding as what now dominates these moors.

33. Porton Down, Wiltshire

Defence, Science & Technology Laboratory

Good old HM Government. They're doing a splendid job of making the Defence, Science and Technology Laboratory (DSTL) near the historic city of Salisbury in Wiltshire sound like a boffin's version of Disneyland.

It's where, we are told, vital research is carried out to ensure that both the UK's military as well as the general public are able to benefit from all of the latest scientific and technological developments that are realised there. Dare I ask, in that case, for a gadget that stops the end of the Sellotape from adhering itself to the roll it is affixed to? Probably not because as you have already suspected, this work is performed with the defence of the realm in mind and is, as a result, performed under the sort of high security on hand that you'd expect of something that is relatively open on the outside, but the very epitome of 'hush hush' on the inside. Put it this way, their milkman left his bill in a place he shouldn't have done in 1983 and they haven't let him out yet.

The most widely held belief about Porton Down is that it is a place where the UK's chemical and biological arsenal is held and that many of the experiments that are carried out both inside and outside are related to making them ever more catchable, virulent and altogether unpleasant to anyone who comes into contact with them. This belief came very much to the public's attention in 2018 following the poisoning and subsequent deaths of three local people, who were all in close contact with the chemical substance known as Novichok. It didn't take long for the blame for the attack to be placed on a couple of Russian agents but, for all that, it took only a little bit longer for someone to suggest that the Novichok might have been sourced at Porton Down, a claim that was rapidly and most emphatically quashed. But it didn't stop myriad conspiracy theories about Porton Down and its role from flaring up.

The UK authorities have long since stated that both the chemical and biological testing programme that had been taking place at Porton Down was closed down in the 1950s and that, rather than producing the deadly toxins required, the work there now focuses on developing swift and effective countermeasures to the threats that are posed by those types of weapon. Yes, they go on to admit, we do produce very small quantities of some chemical and biological agents, but these are only to test the proposed 'antidotes' on and are swiftly and safely disposed of when they are no longer in use. Well that's alright then.

A necessary evil then, and laudable honesty. A case of not being able to fight fire without some fire of your own. But it does beg the question of how easily someone could, if they really wanted to, acquire some of the substances in question including, perhaps, Novichok? It does all sound rather fanciful and the basis of one of those thick paperback novels that men of a certain age like so much (the ones with pictures of submarines, mushroom clouds and scantily dressed women on the front covers), but you can't help but think that with Porton Down so close to Salisbury (just under 9 miles) that it was a connection that was always going to be made and, as in all cases like this, the more the idle speculation is denied, the more people think, 'so it must be true'.

One of the roles that Porton Down has which is connected with public life is the research that is carried out there on infectious diseases, with work done in partnership with both the private and education sectors in developing new products that include vaccines. One example of this is the work that has been carried out on the Ebola virus, a sample of which was brought to Porton Down as long ago as 1976, which is when it was first identified. Numerous tests have been carried out on that sample ever since, one which is kept safe and secure (alongside samples of anthrax and the plague) in conditions that include temperatures that are kept to around minus 80 degrees centigrade. Necessary work that is carried out by, for me, some very courageous people who will be as fully prepared as possible should the worse happen and an outbreak of Ebola occurs in the UK.

On the road to Porton Down.

34. Stockbridge, Hampshire

The Houghton Fishing Club

Fishing, golf and tennis. Three pastimes that are desperate to portray an image as being the sort of pursuits every man and woman can take up, whatever their age and background. Pursuits for the people. Yet you can't help but wonder about what lies beneath the glossy PR spin.

Not when there's a golf course (see 31) right in the middle of one of the most densely packed population centres of England that charges upwards of £200,000 for membership, or a tennis club where the membership fees are comparatively modest (see 39), but where the waiting list consists of over 1,000 hopefuls, many of whom have been, well, waiting for many years.

The sort of thing that drives a very large hole through the concept of 'sport for all'.

But fishing as well? Surely not? This, after all, is the very bastion of equality, a pursuit where young boys and girls with a stick, piece of string and worm can compete on the same terms as someone who has spent hundreds, maybe thousands of pounds worth of equipment, and stand the same chance of catching something (other than a cold) as anyone else.

I'm afraid not, and I'm going to blunt here because no matter how much you might like a spot of fishing and yes, even if you do have a few quid in the bank then, despite all that, you are never going to be a member of the Houghton Fishing Club (HFC) in Hampshire.

It was founded in 1822, a time when some of its more privileged founder members would have thought nothing about sending young children up the chimneys of their country piles. Maybe some of them still think it wouldn't be an unreasonable thing to do today? I jest. Let's face it, the current membership can afford to be a bit sniffy about who they allow to fish on their 13 miles of the River Test, especially when the elected membership counts at just twenty-five lucky people. Although luck does not, of course, come into it. Who and what you are most certainly does, and having blood that is a rich shade of blue running through your veins most certainly does. The cult of 'celebrity' (and I salute them for this, if only more establishments would follow their lead) counts for absolutely nothing here. Indeed, if some flighty TV 'star' turned up at their gates (assuming they were capable of finding their way to them in the first place) along with all the gear and that strange sense of entitlement that constantly orbits them like a little moon and said, 'don't you know who I am?', the membership would immediately respond by saying no before, in the style of C. Montgomery Burns, releasing the hounds.

Legends abound about the club and its ways. One reports that it has a changing area that is exclusively for the use of HRH Prince Charles, while another states that no member may live within 20 miles of the clubs stretch of water lest their close proximity makes them take to the water rather more than they should do. Modesty in all things it would seem, apart from, that is, the joining fee, which is rumoured to be around £50,000.

The River Test rises near the village of Ashe passing, en route, Broadlands, the country home of Lord Louis Mountbatten, before becoming tidal as it meets the River Blackwater near to Southampton Water. It features in the novel *Watership Down* by Richard Adams as the river that the escaping rabbits successfully make their way down by means of a punt. Clever bunnies.

It's just as well none of the Houghton Members saw them as they would likely have impeded their progress as none of them possessed membership.

The River Test. Don't even think about doing a spot of fishing here.

35. Thorney Island, West Sussex

MoD Base & Wildlife Haven

Two important points to make here. Firstly, Thorney 'Island' isn't an island and hasn't been for well over one hundred years, having been reconnected to the mainland after the reclamation of 72 hectares of tidal mudflats towards the end of the nineteenth century. So, any romantic notions you might have of a solitary Robinson Crusoe-like existence amidst the creeks and curlews here will, sadly, have to be abandoned.

Secondly, as picturesque and beguiling as Thorney Island unquestionably is, you can't just pack up the kids, dogs, picnic and your drone into the back of the SUV and tramp around it all day as much of the not-an-island is occupied by the MoD.

That's right. More men and women with guns, and they're not afraid to point them.

Thorney was once home to a remote community of farmers and fisherman who were content to eke a living and get on with their uncomplicated lives from the rich bounty available to them there. That is until a man from the MoD paid a visit to the island in 1935 and decided that it would make a rather fine base for an RAF station. So out went all the farmers and fishermen, while in came all the fitters and airmen to replace them. Numerous RAF squadrons made a temporary home for themselves on Thorney, including No. 164 Squadron who used Hawker Typhoons against enemy shipping in the area; 236 Squadron, who did the same thing, albeit with Bristol Blenheims from 1940 to 1941; and 415 Squadron, who utilised the Handley Page Hampden as a torpedo-bomber aircraft against enemy convoys and shipyards until 1942. Make no mistake about it, RAF Thorney Island was a very busy place indeed. It's a lot quieter today of course, but that doesn't mean the MoD doesn't value the strategic value of the site any less, and the island is currently controlled by the Royal Artillery who have named their part of the site Baker Barracks. They were established in 1986 when the 26th Regiment Royal Artillery moved onto the site which has also been the home to the 47th and 12th Regiment Royal Artillery who have shared Thorney as a home with the 16th Regiment Royal Artillery since 2016.

As you may already have worked out, Artillery Units need a lot of open space around them so they can safely practice the art of firing assorted rockets, mortars and missiles without bringing too much attention to themselves or the work that they do. So, for that reason, although the general public are permitted to access Thorney Island, said access is strictly restricted to the public footpath that circles the entire site. However, even access to that path can be dependent upon the consent of the MoD, so it's probably a good idea, if you do fancy a wander around Thorney, to bring some sort of ID along with you as well as being aware that the peace and quiet of your day may, on occasion, be interrupted by the occasional explosion. But don't let that put you off, it can be a very pleasant few hours indeed (providing you keep to the path) as Thorney, named after the proliferation of hawthorn bushes on the island, is ecologically special enough to be part of the Chichester Harbour Site of Special Scientific Interest, as well as forming part of the Chichester and

Langstone Harbours Special Protection Area. It covers around 2,800 hectares in all, much of which are intertidal mudflats, which have long been recognised as a hugely important area for wildlife. Fortunately, the MoD are a fairly benign custodian of the island and tend not to fire their missile onto the environmentally sensitive areas, although I wouldn't necessarily say the same thing about you and your car, were you to merrily go on your way to places on the island where you shouldn't.

One other thing to bear in mind if you are considering a trip to Thorney Island is that as the footpath that runs around the island is largely on the foreshore, there may be times when it is not accessible due to forces of nature (i.e. strong winds and high tides), rather than any obstacles provided by the armed forces in residence. Thus, all in all, it isn't always the easiest and most accessible place to visit and careful pre-planning in advance should be considered.

A gentle reminder about who is in charge on Thorney Island near Chichester.

36. Trafalgar Square, London

Trafalgar Square Underground Station

I genuinely love the London Underground. There's always, for me, a sense of mystery, even excitement, about descending into the depths of the earth and, if like me, that is one of 'your things' then the tube isn't going to let you down, but it will take you down to some impressive depths below street level; the DLR concourse at Bank station is around 140 feet straight down.

If that doesn't sound all that impressive to you, then please take a trip to your search engine of choice and type in 'Chicago Water Tower'. You might not be too keen on being at the top of that on a windy day, right? Well consider this; the Chicago Water Tower is only a tad over 140 feet high. So now imagine having to dig a hole big enough to completely bury it in. That, good and fair reader, is how far down that part of the London Underground is.

It's obviously a very popular destination for tourists and day trippers, a case of the journey you take in London from point A to point B being as much a part of the sightseeing as some of the more well-known landmarks are. One of which, not unreasonably, might be Trafalgar Square. So, I wonder how many visitors have decided to go and visit Lord Nelson and ended up wondering quite what Underground station they're meant to be heading to, which is understandable. Many London Underground stations are named after the place where they stand, for example if you want to go to St Paul's Cathedral then you head for St Paul's. Likewise, Oxford Street is Oxford Circus, Leicester Square is Leicester Square and Westminster Abbey is Westminster. Simple and logical. The fact that you have to know that you need to alight at Green Park for Buckingham Palace is a bit of an aberration, admittedly, but then the home of HRH is next door to a large, well, green park, so if you apply a little lateral thinking it'll soon make sense.

Thus, if you wish to take a look at Trafalgar Square, then you need to make for Charing Cross station. But that wasn't always the case, as there used to be a London Underground station at Trafalgar Square, one that sat on the Bakerloo Line between Charing Cross and Piccadilly Circus. It's not there now of course and the easy assumption to make is that the station was closed. However, it isn't quite as straight forward as that. The station's 'fate' was decided in the 1970s when the current Jubilee Line was being built. The intention there was to terminate it at the current Charing Cross station which was, at the same time, going to be extensively modernised. This took six years to complete and when a new passenger walkway and escalator link was opened between the site of the old Trafalgar Square station and Charing Cross, the end result was that poor old Trafalgar Square was 'consumed' by the new Charing Cross complex and, in an instance, ceased to exist, even if its infrastructure remained largely intact.

For all of the rather sad end to its history, however, Trafalgar Square Underground Station can still claim to have once been a site that was shut to the public and put under lock and key. This happened in September 1938 when it was temporarily closed in order for some urgent structural work to take place on the part of the tunnel that went under the River Thames (it's probably a fair guess to say that any structural work that takes place in a tunnel that runs under a large tract of water counts as 'urgent'). The station remained closed until just before the start of the Second World War when it reopened and was, like so many other stations, eventually requisitioned as an air raid shelter where, in November 1940, seven people were killed when a bomb fell directly onto the station.

The entire London Underground network contains a total of around forty stations that are no longer in use and are closed off to the general public, a number high enough to warrant a book devoted to them alone. Those that remain hidden away under padlock and key include Down Street (closed in 1932); Wood Lane (1959); Blake Hall (1981) and Aldwych (1994).

Trafalgar Square underground station is no more – all change!

37. Westminster, London

White's Gentleman's Club

Here's a confession. I've always wanted to be a member of a private club, 'gentleman's' or otherwise. It's the thought of sitting in a nice comfortable chair in peace and quiet; just me and my newspaper with, perhaps, a plate of sandwiches and a drink at my side. No phone calls, no emails, no incessant chatter or extraneous noise (other than, perhaps, the ticking of an ancient wall clock) from anyone or anything. What bliss. I can, of course, mimic those conditions a little by disconnecting the phone and barricading myself into my living room. Although having to get my own food and drink first would be a bit of a drag; I'd probably prefer that to being a member of White's Gentleman's Club in London, though, because there'll be little of that much desired peace and quiet there. The testosterone is rumoured to run so thick within its hallowed walls that the place is positively dripping with it, as the well-heeled and even more well connected use it as a bolthole to let off a little of that steam that they always seem to possess in abundance, and usually by means of a little debauchery.

No thanks. I'd rather settle down with a good book. White's, which was founded back in 1693 had its origins as Chocolate and Tea Parlour which immediately gives it a little bit of a genteel image, all clinking china cups and protruding pinkies, but that didn't last for long. It soon became the favourite haunt of the prominent men of the day (ironic how it is labelled as a club for 'gentlemen' when, in truth, I'd guess that hardly any of its members in the subsequent 300 years or so fitted that description in any shape or form), who were able to secure their membership and the utter discretion that went with it via their social standing, rather than how much money they had in the bank. Eton and Oxbridge, Sir? That'll do nicely.

The club's current members are rumoured to include HRH Prince Charles (a respectable double for the heir to the throne therefore, as he is also a member of the Houghton Fishing Club – see 34) as well as his oldest son. Former PM David Cameron was also able to swing membership, helped, no doubt, by the fact that Daddy (Ian Cameron) had been a former club chairman. However, Cameron junior resigned his membership in 2008 in retaliation for the club continuing its policy of not permitting women onto the premises. Women have, on occasion, been allowed past the door with Her Majesty the Queen doing exceptionally well in that regard, having been invited twice – in 1991 and 2016. A group of female protesters then chanced their arms and tried to storm the door in order to gain access in 2018, only to find themselves removed and deposited on the pavement outside, accompanied (no doubt) by a chorus of indignant harrumphing by the dusty old men inside the club at the time.

You won't be allowed in, but should you wish to gaze upon its formidable façade make your way to 37–38 St James's Street in the City of Westminster and look for the Grade I listed building with the Palladian façade. White's consists of five storeys in total, three of which are dedicated for the use of its members. It does not provide any sort of overnight accommodation for them but does boast a member's dining room, a billiards room and a card room and yes, they have a room that has been set aside for a few hands of whist after dinner.

Applying for membership of White's is, as you'd expect, a laborious process. A potential applicant requires a proposer and two seconders, all of whom are, of course, established and respected members of the club. Once this has been done, said application is left in a book in which other members can, if they wish, add their names in support of the would-be member. Once that list has reached a certain number, estimated to be between thirty-five to forty, the application process is speeded up and references are taken up with, it seems, the major quality desired being whether or not the person in question is a 'good chap'. If it transpires that he most certainly is then membership is, eventually, granted, usually for life unless some deep and wicked transgression (asking where the 'toilet' is, for example, rather than the 'loo') is found to have been carried out.

An application for membership cannot be proposed or seconded by the prospective members father, but then who'd want to go out for a good night's quaffing only to see their squiffy dad propping up the bar and moaning about the cricket?

White's Gentleman's Club. Not for me.

38. Whitehall, London

MoD UFO Enquiry Desk

I've known quite a few people who have, in various guises, worked for the MoD. One of them took his role so seriously that he admitted he wasn't even allowed to tell anyone what the colour of the carpet was and has steadfastly kept the secret with him to this day.

You can only conclude that if they are reluctant to divulge the colour of their carpets then they might be even more vigilant about the sort of stuff we'd really like to know about, like, for example, UFOs. What are they all about then? You could ask the question I suppose, but it would likely be met with a blank gaze and a brisk 'we can neither confirm nor deny their existence' before you find yourself waking up on top of a haystack in the middle of Somerset the next day wondering about that really strange dream that you'd just had. Yet, back in 2012, the normally austere *Daily Telegraph* revealed that not only did the MoD welcome news, reports and opinions about UFOs but had even created a role which they called the 'UFO Desk Officer', whose role was to record UFO sightings and even go as far as to investigate up to half a dozen reports of extraterrestrials in the UK that piqued their interest. It's *Men in Black* isn't it? Life imitating art and all that.

They didn't, of course, want their interest in such matters to be taken too seriously. It wouldn't, after all, be that good for their image around the world if rival defence organisations, especially those from potentially hostile nations, had the impression that the top people in the MoD were running around forests in the middle of night looking for ET. So, it was given a relatively soft image of being a post that had been set up in order to communicate with the general public. A nice bit of spin, something that made the MoD appear all soft, fluffy and accommodating. Whereas, of course, in reality, they're (mostly) hardened killers without a molecule of emotions in their collectively hardwired bodies.

There wasn't a great deal of independent research involved. How do we know this? Because one of the MoD staff members openly admitted that they secured most of their source material from Google, nearly 7,000 pages worth infact which, if you take the average word count for a piece of A4 paper as being around 325, means a total of 2,275,000 (yep, that's two million, two hundred and seventy five thousand) words written on the subject. This can only lead to one conclusion; the one that states that for all the informality that surrounded the role, it was, in reality, a topic that the MoD were taking rather more seriously than you might have previously expected. Whichever way you look at it that many pages and words don't really give much credence to the MoD's official stance on the subject, which is that they know of absolutely no evidence to confirm the existence of aliens, spaceships or extra terrestrials in general or, indeed, that they have visited the earth. Note, incidentally, the line is 'they have visited the earth' not that 'they have ever visited the earth'.

One of the daily responsibilities of Whitehall's official UFO desk was to man a hotline which was used by the general public to report sightings, of which there would have been numerous. The MoD staff couldn't, of course, check out every single one and implemented a sensible strategy, which meant that if something unusual was reported by several different witnesses, including some whose profession (i.e. police or airline crew) gave them a certain amount of professional credibility, then the sighting in question would be looked into more closely than one made by a drunken groom to be on the way home from his stag night.

One particularly amusing report (from the Government's own national archive website) that dates back to 1995 stated that, although there was no hard evidence to suggest alien activity in and around the UK, it could be surmised that extraterrestrial visitors, should they arrive, might have one of three reasons to do so (i.e. military reconnaissance, scientific or, and this has tickled me no end – tourism).

I can see the tourism posters on Kepler-452b now. 'EARTH is so BRACING'.

The MoD's mighty London façade.

Rendlesham Forest in Suffolk, the scene of one of England's biggest ever UFO stories.

39. Wimbledon, London

The All England Lawn Tennis & Croquet Club

You've just moved into a nice little apartment in London SW19, and you're the sort of person that likes to keep him or herself relatively fit. Running and swimming isn't on as they're both a little too vigorous for your liking. Tennis, on the other hand, isn't quite so demanding, especially if you play doubles. So yes, the occasional sociable knock with some mates before you all sojourn to a convivial club house afterwards for a plate of sandwiches and a cup of tea all sounds rather splendid, and guess what? You only live 5 minutes away from the agreeably sounding Church Road, where there just happens to be a tennis club with eighteen courts to choose from. So, one of those is bound to be free for, say, 10 a.m. every Tuesday morning?

Dream on. Unless your name happens to be Roger Federer or Serena Williams because, as the popular and oft-quoted rumour has it, it's probably easier to secure membership of this club by winning one of their prestigious titles than it is to do so by more conventional means.

The All England Lawn Tennis & Croquet Club (AELTC) was founded in 1868 by six gentleman fans of croquet, the game which the club was exclusively focused upon until 1875 when a part of their already hallowed lawns was set aside for the increasingly popular game of lawn tennis. Two years later amid a fervour of competitive spirit, the club organised and played its very first Lawn Tennis Gentlemen's Singles Championship, which is now, of course, part of one of the biggest, most prestigious and famous sporting championships anywhere in the world.

'Wimbledon', as it is better known, is the epitome of exclusivity. It has just 375 full members among a total membership of 565, all of whom are divided into five categories, namely Life, Full, Honorary, Temporary and Junior Temporary. The club's membership fees are, perhaps surprisingly, relatively low especially when you compare it to such establishments as the Queenswood Golf Club (see 31), but then money is, for the most part, seen as a rather vulgar thing at Wimbledon where your chances of securing any sort of membership (aside from winning a title) are more to do with the old adage of who you know, rather than what you know. Take, for example, the case of Kate; a nice enough girl. Berkshire born and bred, studied art at university before going onto secure a part time role at a fashion retailer. Respectable, even ordinary, far too ordinary for the AELTC to even consider for anything other than a seasonal job, chauffeuring their pampered players from A to B perhaps, or being made to wear a silly hat and sell overpriced strawberries for a fortnight every year. But nothing more.

That is, of course, until Kate marries the heir to the throne's oldest son and becomes, in an instant, Catherine, Duchess of Cambridge. Membership isn't a problem now, not at all; she's in. Even if she has never as much as held a tennis racket in her life. Comfy seat in the Royal Box ma'am? Thanks very much, don't mind if I do. Such is the way that things are worked out at this particular club.

A range of what the AELTC likes to call 'full privileges' are available to Full and Life Members only. So, if you're Honorary or (shudder) merely Temporary, please leave at once. These privileges include a seat to call your own on Centre Court and full use of all the club's facilities, including all eighteen courts, the gym and of course the famous locker rooms, complete with their marble baths. Once membership is attained, it is highly unlikely that the lucky recipient will ever leave the club, meaning that the space that they currently occupy will only become available as and when they die providing, of course, someone has noticed.

There is exclusive. Then there is elite. Then there is the Houghton Fishing Club (see 34). But, forever lording it right at the top of the exclusive and elite club, will be the AELTC.

The untouchables.

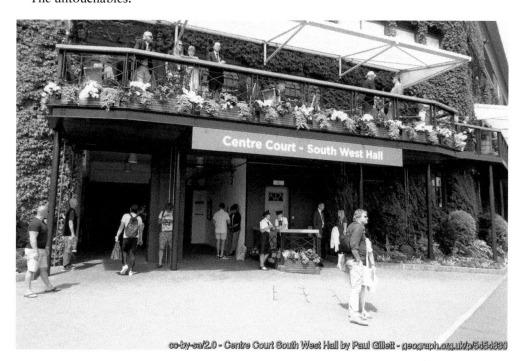

cc-by-sa/2.0 - Centre Court South West Hall by Paul Gillett - geograph.org.uk/p/5454830

Above: Entrance to the South West Hall at Wimbledon.

Right: Fred Perry statue at Wimbledon.

cc-by-sa/2.0 - Sculpture of Fred Perry by Paul Gillett - geograph.org.uk/p/4869900

40. Worsted Lodge, Cambridgeshire

Secure Testing Grounds for Unmanned Drones

Everyone is familiar with a certain online retailer, a giant of the industry who in recent years has dominated retail in the same way a hungry Tyrannosaurus Rex might have bullied its way into an herbivorous dinosaur's picnic. I won't name them here (primarily because they really don't need the publicity) but, suffice to say, it's a brand that is far more well known for being an online behemoth than it is for being the world's largest tropical rain forest. Their latest wheeze is to do away with the perennially chirpy delivery driver and to offer, as an alternative, the delivery of your items by unmanned drone. Now, strictly between me and my readers, I don't think this will come anywhere close to being an option for a number of reasons; the prime one being that I can't see how the drone is going to be able to ring your doorbell and learn to wait the usual one and a half seconds before leaving you a card and clearing off back to the depot. However, the company believe that this is very much a technology they want to master in the next few years so, with that in mind, they have spent a considerable amount of money in building and launching a high-tech testing centre where they can master the art of delivery by drone.

Which isn't, as you might expect, at NASA or Area 51, or even Area 52 for that matter, which is just outside Mansfield incase you're interested. No, it's all happening in a field around 8.5 miles south-east of Cambridge which is already the largest testing facility of its kind in the UK and is closely linked with other sites in the US, Austria and Israel. It will eventually be known as 'Prime Air' with the objective of ensuring that a successful delivery is made within half an hour of the order being placed. It's not an option that is going to be available to all of their customers, indeed, it's probable that if the idea ever does take off (pun intended) only a very small minority of people will ever be able to utilise it, but when has practicality ever been a reason to either do or not do something? There are plenty of examples of various projects being put into place and structures being built simply because the planner wants to prove it can be done, rather than them having any viable purpose, and there's a word for such projects: follies.

Testing at the site began in the summer of 2016, and the clues as to what might be happening at the site were clear. Warnings were issued to local airports and air operators that unmanned aircraft would be flying in the area for, initially, at least a couple of months while, and this was a fringe benefit, Wi-Fi speed in the area shot up as a result of the need for the company to be able to quickly and effectively process the data it was receiving from its drones. Then there were the jobs that suddenly became available at the company's research and development site in Cambridge itself. Clearly, and very obviously, something was going on at the site, yet whenever someone dared to make an enquiry as to what it might be they were met with silence (and this is how much it all piqued interest on a global scale). A reporter from the August NY Times received a 'no comment' in response to his questions. That same reporter went on to mention how his stroll in that part of the normally peaceable Cambridgeshire countryside was interrupted by signs indicating innocent looking fields were, in fact, private property (walkers, generally, are allowed access across farmers' harvested fields in the UK) and, according to a security guard who suddenly appeared from out of the hedgerow, if he didn't move on, the farmer would be called in order to 'evict' him. Then there were the barriers that could be seen in the far distance, not of the unyielding concrete and steel kind but made of straw bales that had been piled up to a height of around 20 feet and behind which, you assume, the oh-so-secret testing was taking place. All very Heath Robinson in design amidst security that you might normally equate to some of the more sinister sites mentioned in this book, rather than for a programme designed to get that DVD you never particularly wanted to you in under half an hour. It also begs another question. Yes, it may well be feasible to prove that a drone can drop off a package in front of a haystack in the middle of a 500-acre field, but how about doing the same thing in a thickly congested street in the middle of London, Paris or New York?

Never going to happen.

cc-by-sa/2.0 - Lane to Worsted Lodge by John Sutton - geograph.org.uk/p/2659510

Above: Rural Worsted Lodge near Cambridge. But beware of men with walkie talkies.

Below: Will this be the scene on your doorstep one day?

Afterword

I am not a historian, and neither is this book any sort of attempt at providing a definitive guide or history of the sites included within its pages.

This book has been inspired by an absolute curiosity of the unknown, the obscure, the hidden and forbidden. The urges to look at and explore places where, for numerous reasons, prying eyes and inquisitive minds have, whether in the past or the current day, either not been welcome or have, for a variety of reasons, simply not been able to see or access the site in question.

If reading about them in here encourages you to do some more detailed research and reading in order to find out more about a particular location's history or purpose, then I will consider that 'job done'. It's a case of my providing you with the notion and you following it through. But be advised, you can't, of course, visit all of the sites in the book, indeed many of them are very definitely off limits to the general public, with very severe sanctions awaiting those who dare to wander where they should not. So, take heed. The book is not an invitation to trespass either and possible arrest and imprisonment may arise as a result of rather too much of that inherent curiosity being shown. It goes without saying that all of the information written in the book is freely available and in the public domain, so if you're here looking for some hitherto unknown secrets, then sorry, but you're in the wrong place!

We're a funny species really. The more lengths we take to keep a secret, the more everybody else wants to know about it.

Writing about some of Britain's more inaccessible and/or secret places has been great fun. I hope you've enjoyed reading about them.

Edward Couzens-Lake
Twitter @edcouzenslake

Acknowledgements

First and foremost, my very sincere and grateful thanks to all at Amberley Publishing for continuing to indulge me as one of their regular authors.

To Doctor Russell Saunders PhD for writing the foreword and being so enthusiastic about science. I've known Russ since we were at Brancaster Primary School together, so we go back a while. He's a top man.

Huge thanks to Penny Mayes and all at www.geograph.org.uk. The site is a fabulous archive of photographs from all over the UK, a national resource we should all treasure and support. Please visit the site and take a look for yourself.

Thanks therefore to all the geograph.org.uk contributors whose photographs have been used in this book:

Given Up (1); Andre Stephens (2); Albert Bridge (4); David Howard (6); Colin Smith (7, 35); Basher Eyre (9); Chris Thomas-Atkin (10); Nick Chipcase (11); Derek Harper (13); Thomas Nugent (14); Becky Williamson (15), Maurice Pullen (15, Frome); Glynn Baker (16), Patrick Mackie (17); Toby Speight (18); Christine Johnson (21); David Howgood (22); James Denham (24); Jim Barton (25); Phillip Halling (26); Nigel Thompson (27); Gerald England (28); Christine Matthews (29); Peter Barwick (31); Neil Theasby (32); Martin Dawes (32, distance view); Phil Williams (33); David Dixon (34); Dr Neil Clifton (36); Anthony O'Neill (37); Robin Sones (38); Simon Leatherdale (38, Rendlesham); Paul Gillett (39) and John Sutton (40).

Shutterstock photo credits to Kev Gregory (3), globalgaz (12), BBA Photography (19, Hampstead), catch-my-eye (19, bridge), Phil Silverman (20) and this_is_beauty (40, drone).

Special thanks to Mark Scott, owner of the Kelvedon Nuclear Bunker, for giving permission to use the photographs of his property, which is well worth a visit. See www.secretnuclearbunker.com.

Other photographic credits to Chris Cotton (5), Camilla van Gerbig and Ian Sporne (30).

I am grateful to Mark Scott of the *New York Times* for his online article 'A Peek at the Secret English Farm Where Amazon Tests Its Drones' (1 October 2016).

If I have made any errors or omissions anywhere in the text or with the photographic credits, rest assured it was most definitely accidental and not intentional. Feel free to contact me so that the relevant corrections can be made in time for future editions of this book.

Edward Couzens-Lake
March 2020

About the Author

Norfolk-born author, features writer and broadcaster Edward Couzens-Lake has written eighteen books to date including a number of autobiographies where he has worked as the subject's ghostwriter.

His works, current and future, include the story of a nurse who recalls her time working in Portsmouth as the city was bombed during the Second World War, as well as the thrilling tale of a former RAF fighter pilot whose service history included flying Harriers in the Falkland Islands and a three year spell spent as a member of the RAF's aerobatic team The Red Arrows.

He has a particular interest in the Cold War period and has written several features relating to it, with particular reference to the military bases and installations that were operating from his native East Anglia at the time.

Edward is also an in-demand copywriter and blogger for a number of individual clients and corporate businesses throughout the UK.

You can find out more about him and his work on his website www.couzenslakemedia.com.